Setting Teams
Up For Success

Kevin Carson
Max Isaac

From 3Circle Partners

3Circle Partners works with businesses that are looking to enhance value by driving better performance and/or maximizing their investments in improvement programs. Our customized approach will accelerate your organization's performance through strong leadership and strategy, solid internal processes for superior execution, and effective interactions.

Acknowledgements

Thanks to Meredith Belbin for his support over the years and allowing us to cite his material. We would also like to thank Sue Reynard and Carole Johnson for their invaluable contributions to this book.

ISBN 0-9735701-5-6

Printed by 3Circle Partners in the U.S.A.
www.3circlepartners.com   Ph: 416-481-0792

Table of Contents

PART II: TEAM EFFECTIVENESS

Preface

We have routinely asked employees of our clients to estimate the percentage of teams they have participated on that have been successful. Their first estimates typically range from 30% to 100%. When we introduce a tighter definition of success, such as *"successful teams are ones which achieve their initial goal or goals, without recourse to additional unanticipated resources (time, money, people),"* the estimates drop consistently into the 25% to 40% range.

Furthermore, when asked to describe why the team has failed, the answers routinely point to factors outside of the team: that goals were not realistic, the team's solution was rejected, a critical support resource (IT for instance) was not available, management changed its mind or focus, team members couldn't devote time to the task due to conflicting priorities, etc. Rarely do the answers they give point towards issues internal to the team or within their immediate control.

Blaming failure on factors outside the team is so consistent a pattern as to be nearly universal. Yes, it's true that some teams are set up for failure based on a lack of sponsor commitment or unrealistic expectations. But even so, the tendency to avoid self-reflection or self-criticism, while present in all of us to some degree, is clearly exaggerated in teams. The lack of team introspection is most likely the reason that many causes of failure or underperformance go both undetected and unaddressed.

When you have a work process that is underperforming, what's the best way to improve it? Use the scientific method to understand, characterize, measure, and analyze the process factors, then take action to make permanent changes. The same approach works for improving how teams work together. This book will show you data-based principles on how to make teams most effective.

Our goals in these discussions are two-fold:

- To move teams as rapidly as possible into peak-performance mode
- To create the conditions under which continuous improvement can occur

You may have heard about the four-phased model of team evolution: Forming-Storming-Norming-Performing. The goal of that model seems to be to make it OK that teams don't work effectively all the time. In contrast, our goal is to give you the information you need to move as quickly as possible into Performance. Paying careful attention to the "science" of team effectiveness will allow you to radically shorten or circumvent the trial-and-error approaches embodied in most teams we encounter.

Continuous improvement is founded on good decision-making, which is what happens only when reliable information is known to and understood by all the people involved in making that decision. It is the goal of this book to help you get the data you need to decide the best way to construct and operate your team. We do this in two parts:

I) Looking at team composition: how to determine the best *combination* of people to serve on the team

II) Creating structures and guidelines that will allow this set of people to work together most effectively

We're not satisfied with a team success rate of only 25%—40%, and bet that you aren't either. The information in this book provides the fundamental building blocks you need to set your teams up for success.

Part I

Team Composition

Introduction

Irene, Carlos, Sandy, and Roger have been brought together in a development team charged with designing a new mortgage service for their bank. Irene, as the bank manager, is serving as the team leader and has selected the other members. She picked Carlos because he knows the most about mortgages, Sandy because she is an experienced loan officer, and Roger because he was involved in several service design projects in the past.

Everything goes well for about a month. The team has lively discussions around setting goals and holds very productive meetings with customers to identify critical needs. But then things go awry. Irene, Carlos, and Roger have come up with several potential service designs, but can't seem to finalize the definition. They keep thinking of more and more different options to build into the service. Sandy, on the other hand, sees time slipping by, but doesn't feel like she can stand up to the other team members to enforce deadlines.

If your company is like this bank, the selection of team members is a straightforward process conducted by a manager or executive. Like Irene, your managers or executives chose teams based on common criteria such as subject matter expertise, possession of relevant skills or knowledge, availability, a personal stake in the outcome of the project, and position within the company.

But is that really the best approach? You've probably seen teams like this one that perform great for a while but then get bogged down—or ones that never seem to get out of the project design phase. The failure of many teams makes it clear that perhaps we should consider whether something else is going on; that perhaps we need to consider whether a given *collection* of individuals will work well together.

In fact, this latter approach does provide insights into what exactly makes an effective team. The study of team composition began back in the 1970s when Meredith Belbin, a researcher in the United Kingdom, spent nine years intensively researching the factors that made teams either effective or ineffective. The outcome of this research is his seminal work on Team Role Theory, which explains why it is the *mix* of different team skills within the team that is the primary determinant of team effectiveness. In research trials, Belbin and his colleagues were able to accurately predict which teams of executives would do well in management simulations and which would falter. The findings have since been applied worldwide to real-life business situations.

For our purposes here, the critical outcome from Belbin's research is that the criteria his research revealed as being crucial to team success bear little to no resemblance to standard team-selection criteria, such as those listed above. More importantly, while the criteria in widespread use have little to no correlation to team success, Belbin's Team Role

Theory has great predictive power. And it shares the virtue of being relatively easy to implement in the real world.

In this section, we will quickly recap Belbin's research then explore its application to you as an individual and to your teams. We'll also explore the experience of Irene's mortgage team in more depth. But first some background.

CHAPTER 1

Belbin's Research: Discovering team roles

Belbin's research was a cooperative effort between Cambridge University and Henley College. Henley had been largely unsuccessful in forming teams that were routinely successful in business simulation games run during executive education seminars. The college contacted Meredith Belbin and commissioned him to undertake a study of what made some teams more successful than others. Over a period of nine years, Belbin studied participants assigned to small teams which competed against each other in a management simulation.

Phase 1: Teams of high intelligence

An early hypothesis was that the success of these *teams* would be highly correlated to the *individual* excellence of team members (that is, the teams with the smartest people would finish highest). As a matter of course, Belbin administered standardized intelligence tests to the students. Based on the information he had on all individuals attending the workshops, he intentionally put those with the highest scores together in teams (dubbed "Apollo" teams after the American space program's rocket scientists).

It may not surprise you that when the results of the simulation games came back, the Apollo teams typically finished close to last or dead last! They were difficult to manage, prone to destructive and unresolved debates, and often more internally competitive than collaborative. In many cases, one individual's actions would intentionally or unintentionally undermine those of another team member.

There were a few successful Apollo teams. Like all Apollo teams, their members were highly intelligent (the definition of an Apollo team), but the people on the successful Apollos tended to be less assertive and there was a dynamic chairman (we'd call him a team leader nowadays) who was able to corral the talents of the team members and also counteract any tendency for members to sit back and be passive. In addition, the successful Apollo teams had explicit conversations about how to compensate for such a uniformly intellectual group. With these factors and strategies in place, they managed to develop and execute effective strategies without devolving into internal squabbling.

Phase 2: Teams of like personalities

The rare successful exceptions to the Apollo pattern became the basis for a shift away from purely intellect-based hypotheses towards ones that incorporated more behavioral elements. As part of his research, Belbin administered personality tests in addition to intelligence tests. "Pure teams" were formed of individuals with like personalities to see if there was any advantage to certain personality profiles.

While there were slight performance differences among the various pure teams, none of them was seen to be universally effective. Rather, their personalities tended to make them well-suited to certain types of tasks and ill-suited to others. That means that during the multi-day management simulation, each of the pure teams' weak points were exposed at some point, and overall the teams were deemed to be less-than-optimal performers.

Phase 3: Searching for balance

The focus of Belbin's investigation now turned to achieving balanced teams that could combine the best attributes of the different "pure teams" without suffering from their inevitable shortcomings in specific instances or activities. Here the challenge was to isolate what attributes were significant contributors to enhanced team performance.

Because the results of the teams were measurable and the composition of team members was known from the standpoint of individual test scores on personality, intelligence and other tests, the researchers were able to analyze what combinations were present in successful teams and absent in failed teams. As the study progressed, Belbin and his team developed descriptions for nine different **team roles**, skills that proved useful on teams. Here is a quick recap of what Belbin discovered about team roles:

One of the first critical attributes to emerge in the research was **creativity,** which was fulfilled by two distinct types of people:

- Highly creative individuals came to be called **Plants** by Belbin because he intentionally "planted" them into teams. When these individuals were given the opportunity by the team to be creative, the team's performance consistently improved. In other cases, the Plant was suppressed or overlooked, and the team failed to harness the power of their creativity.

- A second category associated with new ideas is **Resource Investigator**. The differentiation is that while Plants rely on their own internal thinking to come up with ideas, Resource Investigators talk to other people (often outside the team) to collect new ideas or discover opportunities that the team could incorporate into their strategies and actions.

Whether or not a team is able to capture ideas supplied by Plants or Resource Investigators seems to hinge on how it is managed by its leader or chairman. Again, Belbin found this role being filled by two different types of people for two very different reasons:

- The more successful chairmen had a specific set of attributes that were later embodied in a role called **Coordinator**. These individuals are seen to be trusting and accepting of others, dominant, committed to goals, as well as calm in a crisis. These traits allow them to guide and facilitate the group effectively, as well as to orchestrate the assignment of tasks to the best-suited individuals.

- Another role that emerged during this phase, that of **Monitor Evaluator,** proved to be a vital contributor to team success. People with this capability are serious-minded and largely immune to infectious enthusiasm. They prefer to thoroughly think matters through issues before coming to a decision. They are often the only ones able to hold their ground against a Plant. The Monitor Evaluator can discover hidden flaws in an argument, enabling them to convince Plants to change their minds.

Another key role that emerged were the people who made sure that things got done. The **Implementer** is practical, realistic, and self-sacrificing, ensuring that necessary tasks are performed. They are disciplined, orderly, and skilled at planning. Their presence on a team ensured that decisions made would be turned into results.

Another style of leadership that Belbin identified only after his research became more widely known has been dubbed **Shaper,** a role that is in many ways the opposite of the collaborative Coordinators. Shapers are direct, argumentative, challenging, and prone to aggression, yet they are good humored about it all and seem to relish the conflict itself. Shapers are seen to be the cure for lackadaisical teams but could be a disruptive force within otherwise harmonious teams.

The presence of decidedly different personalities and styles in a team inevitably leads to interpersonal conflicts, in some cases so extreme that two individuals are "toxic opposites" and cannot work together. In other cases, some individuals get overlooked or shut out. The antidote to these pitfalls rests in a role called the **Team Worker**, who would often make a timely intervention to restore balance to the team process. Team Workers are socially and politically adept, but not dominant. The have a lubricating effect on teams, maintaining morale and rapport within the team.

Two final roles that emerged are:

- **Completer Finisher**: Detail-oriented by nature, these people have a desire to see things through to the end. They serve to ensure both the completion of tasks and that quality standards are met.

- **Specialist:** While not a significant factor in the management simulation game, the role of Specialist was of critical significance when Belbin began applying the theory to real-world settings. In real situations, there is often a need for specialized, expert-level knowledge, without which the team would certainly fail. By nature, the Specialist relentlessly pursues additional knowledge on a narrow front until they have mastered the subject.

The descriptions of these nine roles are summarized in Table 1.A (next page). In addition, there is a quick reference guide to all nine roles at the end of this section.

Table 1.A: Summary of Teams Roles

Role	Contribution
Plant (PL)	Creative, imaginative, unorthodox. Solves difficult problems.
Monitor / Evaluator (ME)	Sober, strategic and discerning. Sees all options. Judges accurately.
Specialist (SP)	Single-minded, self-starting, dedicated. Provides knowledge and skills in rare supply.
Shaper (SH)	Challenging, dynamic, thrives on pressure. Has the drive and courage to overcome obstacles.
Implementer (IMP)	Disciplined, reliable, conservative and efficient. Turns ideas into practical actions.
Completer / Finisher (CF)	Painstaking, conscientious. Searches out errors and omissions. Delivers on time.
Resource Investigator (RI)	Extroverted, enthusiastic, communicative. Explores opportunities. Develops contacts.
Team Worker (TW)	Cooperative, mild, perceptive and diplomatic. Listens, builds, averts friction, calms the waters.
Coordinator (CO)	Mature, confident, a good chairperson. Clarifies goals, promotes decision-making, delegates well.

Team Roles vs. Team Size

Belbin's rule does NOT mean that a team must be composed of nine individuals, each playing one role. As noted above, most of us are capable of being effective at more than one role. For the sake of simplicity, let us assume that an individual can play three of the nine roles very well (this capability is not unusual). It would be theoretically possible then to have a balanced team with as few as three people.

However, in practice the optimal size is from five to seven individuals. With less than five people, a team is likely to have voids, or unfilled team roles. With more than seven, the roles are usually all covered, but surpluses become commonplace. (We will cover the problems associated with voids and surpluses in greater detail in Chapter 2.) Furthermore in teams that have more than seven members, the sense of team tends to break down. Often once a team reaches around ten people, "inner circles" tend to form as team members naturally gravitate back to a more functional size.

Validation of the Belbin Model

The proof of a theory is its reliability and predictive capability. Belbin's theory that a team composed in a balanced fashion will generally outperform an imbalanced one was tested in multiple iterations of the management simulation. The results of two series of trials—the first in 1976 and the second in 1979—are shown in the graphs on the next page.

Figure 1.1: Results of Belbin's Research

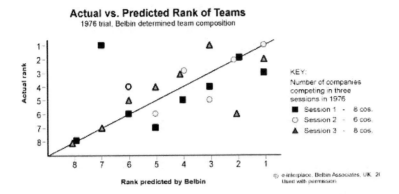

Actual vs. Predicted Rank of Teams
1976 trial. Belbin determined team composition

KEY:
Number of companies
competing in three
sessions in 1976
■ Session 1 - 8 cos.
○ Session 2 - 6 cos.
▲ Session 3 - 8 cos.

© e-interplace. Belbin Associates, UK. 2(
Used with permission

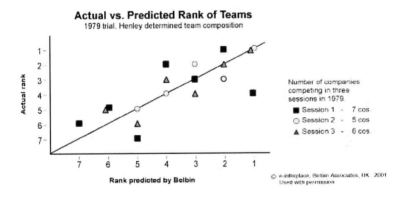

Actual vs. Predicted Rank of Teams
1979 trial. Henley determined team composition

Number of companies
competing in three
sessions in 1979
■ Session 1 - 7 cos
○ Session 2 - 5 cos
▲ Session 3 - 6 cos

© e-interplace, Belbin Associates, UK. 2001
Used with permission

The comparison between these graphs is interesting because in 1976, Belbin himself selected the teams based on the results of his research, while in 1979, he made the predictions *after* the teams were already selected by others. As you can see, Belbin's predictions were remarkably accurate. There isn't a perfect correlation between the prediction and actual results in either case, but in most cases, teams finished within one or two ranks of the prediction. Furthermore, in the cases of discrepancies, anecdotal evidence gathered in interviews indicated that while the team was balanced "on paper," they were not so in practice. One of the critical roles that an individual should have been playing was in fact not performed, either because of the way the team organized itself or because the individual chose to contribute in some other way.

Belbin's Team Role Theory gives a company much more predictive power (and thus control) over team effectiveness than is possible with other methods. These results established Belbin as a world leader in behavioral science research.

CHAPTER 2

Applications of Belbin's Insights

Because Belbin's research was focused on teams, our major application of his theory will reside at that level. However, we have found that the ideas that help individuals best contribute to teams also have profound implications to their daily jobs. As a result, we will divide our application discussions into team and individual topics. We'll talk first about how to analyze the team role strengths for individual team members, then how teams and individuals can apply that information.

Developing Team Role Profiles

The analysis of where a team is strong or weak starts by having each member do a **Team Role analysis,** which is a combination of ratings they give themselves and that others give them on skills related to the nine roles. Each person completes a questionnaire that asks about how they deal with different situations; four to six others (called Observers by Belbin) also evaluate that person on what behaviors they see the person displaying in the workplace. A software package analyzes the results, and gives a report showing the rank order of team role skills exhibited by that person. Figure 2.1 shows one such report.

Figure 2.1: Belbin Team Role Profile

	1	2	3	4	5	6	7	8	9
				Team Roles in Rank Order					
Self-perception	ME	CF	IMP	SH	SP	CO	PL	RI	TW
Observer #1	ME	CF	PL	IMP	CO	SP	TW	RI	SH
Observer #2	CF	IMP	PL	ME	CO	SP	SH	TW	RI
Observer #3	CF	ME	CO	SP	IMP	PL	TW	SH	RI
Observer #4	CF	PL	TW	SP	CO	ME	SH	IMP	RI
OVERALL RANKING	CF	ME	PL	IMP	SP	CO	SH	TW	RI

The answers to the self-ratings showed that this person thought they were strongest as a Monitor Evaluator. Only one of the four Observers also rated that person high on ME skills; another rated them highly enough in that category that it ended up second overall. Everyone agreed this person did not show strong skill as a Resource Investigator (it fell 8th or 9th on each ranking). The overall ranking of skills for this person is shown at the bottom.

The relative strengths of roles varies from person to person. We have seen Team Role analyses of individuals that show just one very strong role and every other role being very weak. This is unusual but, clearly, not impossible. Most often, there are several roles that a person and his observers agree are very prominent, and several roles that emerge as being rather weak, leaving a middle group in which the person is not exceptionally strong or weak. As we examine the composition of teams we often find it convenient to divide the nine roles into three groupings in the following manner:

- The top three ranked skills for any person are considered their strengths or **preferred roles.** These behaviors come most easily or naturally to the person and are what they will be best at. The preferred roles for the person shown in Figure 2.1, for example, are Completer Finisher, Monitor Evaluator, and Plant.

- The middle three skills (overall ranking of four through six) are called **manageable**: although performing those skills or behaviors doesn't come quite as naturally as preferred skills, the person can often fulfill those roles competently, especially on a short-term or situational basis. For the person in Figure 2.1, they would not naturally show Implementer, Specialist, or Coordinator skills very often if left to their own inclinations, but could do so if the situation called for those skills.

- The bottom three roles are tasks that the person is weakest in and are called **least preferred roles.** Asking a person to perform behaviors associated with least preferred roles will put them under great stress. The person in Figure 2.1 would have a very hard time acting as a Shaper, Team Worker, or Resource Investigator, and probably would not perform very well in those roles.

Note, as stated above, the division into sets of three must be checked carefully. Some people may have only one or two preferred roles, with more manageable or least preferred roles making up the difference.

> ### The flipside of strengths: Allowable weaknesses
>
> The factors that determine a person's strengths also lead to inherent weaknesses that are unlikely to be changeable in the short or even medium term. Where roles are heavily influenced by personality (e.g., Resource Investigators typically are somewhat to very extroverted), attempts to fix a weakness often serve to destroy the associated strength while having only a slight beneficial impact on the weakness being targeted. Thus attempting to rein in a highly extroverted RI would probably place a strain on that person and would probably harm their ability to network and do the things RI's are good at. We'll talk more about dealing with allowable weaknesses later in this chapter.

Team Applications

The Belbin methodology can be used either proactively (to help shape team composition) or reactively (as a diagnostic tool when problems arise). There are many situations in which there is very little opportunity to actually change team composition. In these cases the Belbin approach can be extremely effective in bringing about an awareness of the imbalances that exist. Once recognized, a team can develop effective strategies to address team imbalances.

Roles needed during project phases

Different team roles take on additional significance during different phases of a project. As shown in Table 2.A for example:

- Shapers and Coordinators are particularly important when a team is working on confirming customer needs and goals for the team
- Plants and Resource Investigators are critical when coming up with the creative ideas for meeting those needs
- When a team needs to develop plans, the skills of Monitor/Evaluators and Specialists are in greatest demand
- If team success relies on making connections outside the team, the team should call on its Resource Investigators and Team Workers
- Keeping the team organized and on track is best done by Implementers and/or Coordinators
- To make sure that all plans are carried through to the last detail, the team needs the skills of Completer/Finishers and Implementers

Table 2.A: Importance of Roles Varies by Project Phase

Needs	SH	CO	
Ideas	PL	RI	
Plans	ME	SP	
Contacts	RI	TW	
Organization	IMP	CO	
Follow Through	CF	IMP	

Teams that aren't aware of how to match different needs with different team roles often muddle through calling on anyone in the team to do any kind of work. At best, that approach is inefficient. At worst, it can spell increased stress and disaster as people are called on to perform tasks to which they are ill-suited.

Interpreting Balance and Imbalance

The other main application of team role knowledge is dealing with imbalances in team composition. Belbin proved that balanced teams perform better over the long run than imbalanced ones. Specifically, what is required is that each of the nine roles is represented on a team. Table 2.A explains why: while at any given point a team's tasks may not require that all nine roles be present, every role *is* needed over the long haul as a team's needs change. (The potential for temporary success of imbalanced teams was borne out by Belbin's imbalanced "pure teams" which did quite well at selected tasks, but which failed over the longer run.)

Teams may be imbalanced in two ways:

- A role may not be represented on the team (a **team role void**): The consequence of a team role void is that at some point, the absent role will be in demand and there will be no one filling it. This team's struggles will be quite predictable: For example, if the team lacks a Shaper, it may be slow to action. If it lacks a strong Plant, it may not develop the best possible strategies.

- A team may be over-represented (a role **surplus**): This situation carries its own pitfalls. These teams will often devolve into internal competition as the members who are strong in the same roles try to outdo one another in the same role. A team filled with Plants, for example, is likely to become immersed in ideas at the expense of addressing practical realities. Plants tend to feel significant ownership of their own ideas and this can often lead to "idea competition" which hampers convergence in thought and subsequent conversion of the ideas into action. Shaper-heavy teams will argue over goals, and power struggles will quickly break out. Members on surplussed-teams tend to overindulge the activities that line up with the surplus role. In a Plant team, brainstorming is fun for the team members, so they continue to do it long after the point of diminishing returns. These teams often take on the worst characteristics of the role that is in surplus.

Analyzing a team's balance

To tell whether there are voids or surpluses, the team needs to create a map that compiles the rankings for each team member by filling in a form like that shown in Figure 2.2.

Figure 2.2 Format for Team Role Map

Team Role		Team Member A	Team Member B	Team Member C	Team Member D
Thinking	Plant				
	Monitor Evaluator				
	Specialist				
Action	Shaper				
	Implementer				
	Completer Finisher				
People	Resource Investigator				
	Team Worker				
	Coordinator				

The results are then analyzed by comparing the ranks of various roles across all team members. One example is shown on the next page (Figure 2.3), along with the conclusions that can be drawn from it.

Figure 2.3: Map of Team Role Rankings

	Person A	Person B	Person C	Person D	Person E	Person F
PL	7	7	2	4	9	8
ME	4	2	4	1	4	2
SP	5	3	5	5	8	1
SH	3	1	1	2	7	3
IMP	8	4	9	8	2	5
CF	1	9	6	7	6	6
RI	6	5	8	9	5	7
TW	2	6	7	6	1	9
CO	9	8	3	3	3	4

This team map shows the Belbin results for a team of six people (labeled a to f in the figure). Person A, for example, had a strong preference for being a Completer Finisher, Team Worker, and Shaper as shown by the rankings 1, 2, 3 in that column; that person was weakest in Plant, Implementer, and Coordinator capabilities, as shown by the rankings of 7, 8, 9. Ideally, you want to have at least one 1, 2, or 3 in each of the roles (showing that the role will be represented well on the team)—but not too many high numbers for any role.

As can be seen in the map above, there are many 1s, 2s, and 3s in the Shaper role meaning this team has a surplus of those capabilities. Conversely, there are only scores of 5 and lower in the Resource Investigator role; this a void. Left to its own devices, the team would probably have a great deal of Shaper-induced conflict: arguing over direction and goals, struggles amongst the Shapers to lead the meetings and the team, etc. The lack of Resource Investigators could also pose problems in that the team would not have an outward focus, possibly becoming insular and/or failing to communicate or manage their external contacts effectively.

The other roles seem to be fine, with the possible exceptions of Coordinator (CO) and Monitor Evaluator (ME), both of which have borderline team role surpluses. The ME concentration is more problematic than that of CO, due to the higher ranking of the preferred roles (ranks are 1,2, and 2 for ME versus 3,3,and 3 for CO). Also, the fact that the lowest ranking for anyone in the ME role is #4 can cause issues. A team with an ME surplus would tend toward overanalysis, potentially leading to paralysis by analysis. In this particular team, paralysis is probably unlikely to occur because the Shapers would quickly become impatient for results.

Dealing with imbalances

Only about 10% of teams will be balanced perfectly (no voids, no surpluses, each role having at least one high rank), assuming that they are made up of six randomly chosen members.

The good news is that the remaining 90% of the teams that are formed without considering role balance and which have some structural issues can almost all be made effective. There are a few cases (roughly 5% of the time), where the team is so imbalanced that a change in membership may be the only way to adequately restore balance in the team.

Addressing voids: Determine which team member has the missing role as a manageable one (that is, it ranks 4, 5 or 6 in the assessment). Thereafter, when that role is needed the individual will have to make a team role sacrifice away from their preferred roles and into the scarce one. This should be sustainable, provided that role is not required to be played on a continual basis. Normally in project teams this will not be an issue as the team will meet infrequently, and the person making the sacrifice will have ample opportunity outside of these meetings to revert to more preferred roles. A key success factor in this strategy is that the rest of the team recognize the need for the sacrifice and be supportive of the team member making the sacrifice: allow them to consciously focus on filling the scarce team role by taking on some of the workload, etc.

Dealing with surpluses: Surpluses are more difficult to deal with than voids. In some cases, it will be sufficient for the team members with a preference for the surplus role to merely throttle back their attempts to play it. This will often work in situations where the team members are not deeply emotionally involved in the debate. However, this is often difficult as the preferred role feels good or fun; as a result it is very hard to not indulge it. A more commonly successful strategy is for the team to firmly establish one or two of the members who will play the lead role for the surplus team role. It will then be necessary for the others with that preferred role to consciously avoid it completely, often by focusing on another preferred or manageable team role. It may also be necessary for the team to empower one member of the team who does not have the surplus role as a preferred role to be the monitor of team activity and to "raise the flag" when the team has inadvertently devolved into unproductive indulgence of that role.

Balancing in action

Irene's mortgage service design team had their Belbin profiles developed. They discovered that three of the members—Irene, Carlos, and Roger—all have Plant as a preferred role while Sandy is a strong Completer/Finisher. Irene is also a strong Resource Investigator; Carlos and Roger are both specialists (though in different areas, fortunately). None on the team are strong in Shaper tendencies.

Given this profile, it is not surprising that the team bogged down in the design phase, when the surplus of Plant tendencies dominated. The three most assertive members of the team were unwilling to leave behind the creative phase. This problem was exacerbated by the void of a Shaper, which meant there was no one who would plunge a stake in the ground and say "let's just do it."

It was impractical to add new people to the team at this point, so the team discussed other options for getting past the problem areas. To get out of the churn from having too many Plants, Irene did her best to act like a Shaper when required, pushing the team towards action. (It was difficult for her because she didn't relish conflict as most Shapers do.) Roger also focused on his Implementer strengths, helping them get them out of the design phase and into planning.

To reduce the stress on team members who were required to play their manageable or even least-preferred roles, the team set up a ground rule that acknowledged which roles were missing on the team, encouraging them all to try to notice when that role was needed and step in to fill it as necessary.

The situation faced by this team is typical of what you'll encounter on your own teams. There will likely be too many people strong in a few roles and not enough who are strong in other roles. In some cases, the best recourse is to change team membership so that all roles are represented, but as noted above that is not always possible or even necessary.

The best strategy overall is to acknowledge what roles are missing and decide who will fill those voids. Look first at people for whom the roles are manageable; as a last resort turn to someone for whom the role falls into the least preferred category.

Often, just the awareness of having a surplus of one role will help deal with the issue of having too many team members making similar contributions. Having a number of Plants, for instance, may not be a problem if there is an explicit plan to deal with the idea competitiveness on the team that is often present when there is a surplus of Plants. Our experience suggests that teams need to make sure their vigilance against the offending behavior must be maintained or it may subtly creep back as individuals revert to their usual patterns of behavior.

Individual Applications

There are several ramifications of Belbin's research for individuals as well as teams. The three primary impacts for the individual lie in self-management:

- **Role playing:** what role to play in a certain setting
- **Coherence:** making sure that how you see yourself matches how others see you
- **Allowable weaknesses:** how to handle the weaknesses that are the flipside of strengths

Role playing

Role-playing is a situational exercise conducted at the individual level. As we saw from the team mapping discussion above, there are certain situations in which it may be advisable or even essential for the individual to shift away from their preferred roles. However, Belbin's advice to individuals is that this should be the exception rather than the rule. The general rule is to play to your strengths (preferred roles should be sought out), and avoid your weaknesses (least preferred roles should be delegated to others).

The reasoning behind this advice is that, to a great degree, an individual's preferred team roles are rooted in deeply embedded behavior patterns. While the need for various roles on the team will change over time and team members will have to shift between their preferred (and perhaps even manageable) roles, the reality is that at any point in time a person is most likely to be successful if they are engaged in activities that play to their strengths and make their weaknesses irrelevant.

What typically occurs when we stray into our least preferred roles is that we set ourselves up for failure or at the very least a great deal of stress with mediocre results. Attempts to play the weaker roles often come across poorly to the rest of the team as well, leading to lowered trust and increased interpersonal conflict. Stress is a feeling of anxiety based in being unable to cope with a situation. This definition seems to line up nicely with what Belbin's least preferred roles represent. Asking a non-Plant to be creative and unorthodox will be unlikely to generate much creativity but will almost certainly put that individual on the spot and under quite a bit of stress.

Once you know your own team role profile, it is your responsibility to actively seek out opportunities where your strengths will be valued contributions, and manage situations so that you are not requested or required to act in areas where you are weak. (The basic formula suggested by Belbin's research maximizes both an individual's contribution to team success and the individual's own personal success.)

It is also your responsibility to be alert for situations when you need to shift between roles. In our mortgage team, for example, Irene realized that she had to temporarily abandon one of her preferred roles, that of Plant, in order to allow the team to make progress. Roger did the same thing, focusing on where he could contribute in an Implementer role and suppressing his natural Plant capabilities.

Coherence

Coherence is the degree to which you see yourself as others see you. This attribute is almost universally present in people identified as great leaders. It is embodied in adjectives commonly used to describe admired leaders like genuine, authentic, transparent, self-aware, mature, consistent. Coherence more strongly correlates with effective leadership than any of the nine team roles—meaning that role which a person plays is less important than how well that person knows and plays to their strengths and manages their weaknesses.

Having coherence makes it very easy to accurately place a person into suitable tasks; no guessing is required. Also, coherent individuals are generally viewed as easy to deal with because they are predictable and consistent. At an interpersonal level, coherence allows other people to more quickly understand who we are and avoid inadvertently offending us because our true nature is more quickly and consistently visible.

The benefit to an individual of becoming more coherent is that more of the time in the workplace will be spent on tasks to which they are well-suited. This will naturally allow them to shine more frequently and garner rewards and recognition. On the other side, they will more often avoid tasks to which they are ill-suited, thereby avoiding career or reputation damaging incidents.

Allowable Weaknesses

That weaknesses exists is obvious; what may be less obvious is whether the weakness is "allowable" in the sense that the team or individual should just accept the weakness and find ways to counteract it through other roles on the team, or if it is "disallowable" and the person has to find a way to change that behavior.

Judging this issue relies on what impact the weakness will have on the team and whether compensations can be made for it. The absent-mindedness that may accompany creativity in the Plant role can be compensated for by other roles' strengths, for instance the detail-oriented CF. It is a matter of degrees: if the Plant forgets to come to a meeting that would be disallowable, but merely becoming lost in thought and distracted during a meeting would usually be permissible.

Generally, the weaknesses attached to preferred team roles should be accepted, but consciously managed by the person so that they do not become disallowable. The worst approach is often to try to fix or eliminate them completely; this merely kills the flowers along with the weeds. Often the best way to manage a weakness will involve seeking out a complementary role in another person that inherently offsets the weakness and trying to work collaboratively with that person so that the weakness never comes to the fore-front.

Does Belbin knowledge really make a difference?

Quite often, the insights gained from a Belbin analysis have a profound effect on people. As proof, we offer the following real-life case studies (names of people and companies have been changed for privacy reasons):

Case #1: Nick

Nick was a middle-aged manager who had a lot of experience in project management and a very successful career. Though he had good people skills in general, he had noticed over the years that there were occasional disconnects within the teams he led. By profession he was an accountant, which required him to be very detail oriented and very focused (though by career path, he was now a manager, required to be very strategic in his thinking).

Team members sometimes thought of Nick as micro-managing because he'd try to take over anything analytical. He'd often take on a lot of tasks because he was "the boss." At the same time, the team knew he wasn't the greatest at following through on details, so sometimes tasks would not get done on time.

Nick's perception of himself was as a "super" Monitor Evaluator, always thinking strategically, looking at options, making shrewd judgments about how to get work done. He thought that one of his weakest skills was at the creative end, in what Belbin classifies as a Plant.

To his surprise, other people's perceptions were almost the exact opposite: they rated him as mediocre or moderate at best in Monitor Evaluator skills and very high in the Plant abilities. (Everything else in his profile aligned between his self-perception and the perception of others; the difference in ME and PL scoring was the only glaring discordance.)

This was an "a ha" moment for Nick. The more he thought about it, the more he realized that other people's perceptions were more accurate than his own. He really wasn't that good at the kind of patience and attention required to be a good Monitor Evaluator. And conversely, he really enjoyed the divergent thinking that comes naturally to Plants.

Over the next year, Nick focused very deliberately on developing his creative side. At first, he even asked his teammates to tell him when he was being creative so he could start to recognize his own Plant-ness (so to speak). Coupled with his good people skills, it turned out his true strengths were Plant, Resource Investigator, and Coordinator. So he would come up with creative ideas, not only on his own but also by making connections with many other people, as is typical of an RI. His Coordinator skills were very useful in the early stages of a project, when it was critical that the team get organized around what it needed to accomplish.

Nick learned that he really needed to be paired with Completer Finishers and Implementers if anything was going to get done well and on time! He also became adept at switching roles: serving on a team that happened to have a lot of Coordinators and Plants, he would even slip into his fourth strongest role, Team Worker—meaning he would not try to take control as much as make sure that everyone got a chance to contribute.

As the year passed, Nick realized that his teams were working together better than ever before, achieving better results with greater contributions from all involved. Nick also found that his workday was much less stressful. And he's never looked back from there.

Case #2: June

In some ways, June's story is the opposite of Nick's. When she went through the Belbin analysis, it turned out she had a very coherent profile: that the way she perceived herself was the same way that others perceived her—as a good Implementer. There was one slight difference however: other people also recognized that her strong people skills would make her a good Coordinator, but that wasn't something June had ever thought she could do. Coordinators are often leaders within a group, whether formally or informally, and have a certain confidence that allows them to fulfill that role well.

As June thought about this more, she realized that her contentment with being an Implementer was limiting her career. In order to grow professionally and personally, she decided she would muscle up the nerve to try being a Coordinator. She began being more deliberate and assertive in making sure the pieces of her teams meshed well together. She flourished in this new role, taking on more and more leadership responsibilities over time.

Case #3: Pete

Pete had a meteoric career in sales, quickly rising to the top and staying there for a number of years. Another company recognized his success by offering him the chance to manage sales in one of its divisions. Pete jumped at the chance for career advancement. He approached his new job with enthusiasm, eager to prove himself an able leader.

Unfortunately, things didn't go well at first. After a few months, his division had fallen to having the worst sales performance of any in the company. Because Pete's total compensation was heavily tied to the division's sales performance, he was now making less than half of his previous income at his previous employer. The future was looking quite bleak when Pete had the chance to attend a Belbin seminar. That's when the light bulbs began coming on.

He realized that he had been equating "leadership" with what Belbin called the Coordinator role—which was one of his weakest areas. He had far too short an attention span, did not really enjoy detailed follow-up, and tended to dominate meetings. That was why his team was constantly behind and people felt they weren't given a chance to contribute.

One of Pete's first moves when he returned to the office was to hire a strong Coordinator as his second-in-command. With that person in place and playing the CO role, Pete focused more on what he did well, connecting with resources and opportunistically pursuing new leads (the RI role). In a remarkably short timeframe, his team's performance made a complete turnaround, becoming the most successful division in the company. Pete returned to a happier worklife and his income more than tripled from its low point.

Conclusion

As you've just seen, knowledge of Belbin strengths and weaknesses can have a huge effect on both your own personal and professional development and the success of your teams.

Initiating a project without consideration of team composition is a classic failure mode seen throughout companies today. The Belbin Team Role Theory can be applied to both diagnose existing teams and to design new ones from scratch. It is the diagnosis and identification of countermeasures that lies at the heart of consistently successful project teams and project leaders. It has been our experience that projects can be shortened by the judicious use of team composition techniques because it eliminates wasted effort or indecision—to say nothing of improved quality of results or the more positive experiences of the team members.

Team Roles

Quick Reference Guide

Plant

Characteristics

Plants are innovators and inventors and can be highly creative. They provide the seeds and ideas from which major developments spring. Usually they prefer to operate by themselves at some distance from the other members of the team, using their imagination and often working in an unorthodox manner. They tend to be introverted and react strongly to criticism and praise. Their ideas may often be radical and may overlook practicalities.

They are independent, clever and original. They may be weak in communicating with other people, especially those operating on a different wavelength.

Role on a Team

The main contribution of a Plant is to generate new pro-posals and to solve complex problems. Plants are often needed in the initial stages of a project or when a project is failing to progress. They are prone to divergent or tan-gential lines of reasoning which can be counterproductive in some settings.

A Plant in action

Showing strengths

During a product strategy meeting, Norma sits and listens as two vice presidents argue over which of two products to have the sales force focus on selling. One VP supports Product A because of its greater initial profitability. The other supports Product B because early marketing reports show a lot of potential though its costs are expected to be higher. The two argue back and forth for some time. Norma appears indifferent, doodling on her notepad.

Finally one of the VPs addresses her. "Norma, are you paying attention? What do you think?"

Norma puts down her pen. "Yes, I've been listening. And it occurs to me that maybe we're missing something," she says. "I think if we reconfigured our production lines, we could redistribute our overhead costs and sell both product A and B more profitably without overburdening our sales force. The three dive into the numbers and production strategies more deeply and realize that Norma is right.

> COMMENT: *This is typical Plant behavior, listening closely to data and arguments (even if it doesn't look like they are!), and thinking through the issues carefully before coming up with a new idea that hadn't occurred to anyone else.*

Showing a weakness

At a later meeting, Norma and the two vice presidents are presenting their recommendation to the president of their division. He starts peppering Norma with questions: "What timeframe are we looking at to make these changes? What will it take to get it done? Is this really practical?"

Norma can't answer any of those questions. She loves the creative work, but loses interest once the talk focuses on how to get something done.

> COMMENT: *Though some Plants also have Implementer tendencies, most don't pay much attention to practical issues of feasibility or deadlines. That's allowable as long as you have someone on the team who does care about those issues. You might also need to develop ways to regularly remind a Plant of deadlines or other practical matters.*

Monitor Evaluator

Characteristics
Monitor Evaluators are serious-minded, prudent individuals with a built-in immunity from being over-enthusiastic. They are slow to make decisions, preferring to think things over fully. Usually they have a high critical-thinking ability. They have a capacity for shrewd judgments that take all factors into consideration. A good Monitor Evaluator is seldom wrong.

To many outsiders, the Monitor Evaluator may appear as dry, boring or even overly critical. Many occupy strategic posts and thrive in high-level positions. In some jobs, success or failure hinges on a relatively small number of crunch decisions; this is ideal territory for a Monitor Evaluator.

Role on a Team
Monitor Evaluators are best suited to analyzing problems and evaluating ideas and suggestions. They are very good at weighing the pros and cons of different options. They are often slow to act or speak and may be quieter than other members of the team, so care must be taken to pull them into lively debates.

A Monitor Evaluator in action

Showing strengths
A strategic team is discussing the idea of consolidating office locations. Three of the participants are very enthusiastic, seeing a wealth of possibilities for saving on overhead and achieving other efficiencies. The plans are well underway when Marty speaks up.

"Hold on everybody," he says, "I think we're getting way ahead of ourselves." There's sudden quiet in the room and the energy level drops precipitously. "It seems like you're gung-ho on closing the Sullivan office, but that's also the home of our biggest customer and we have those tax incentives from the city. I don't think they're going to be too happy about that. We really need to explore some more options here before making a decision."

The rest of the team immediately saw that Marty was right in his assessment. Though disappointed at having to regroup their focus, they realized it was good thing he'd stopped them before they got too far down the line.

> COMMENT: *Monitor Evaluators always have an eye towards the larger strategic picture surrounding decisions, and want to get a lot of information before making a final call.*

Showing a weakness

At the next meeting of this team, one of the Resource Investigators on the team reports that she's talked to the customer and moving the office wouldn't be a big deal to them. But Marty shows them data on the impact of losing the tax incentive for those operations, and its much bigger than anyone anticipated. Still, the team decides to go ahead with the consolidation. Marty's reaction, "when this goes bust, don't blame me."

> COMMENT: *Monitor Evaluators have a tendency to sound skeptical (if not cynical). Marty's team had learned to appreciate his strategic insights and ignore his occasional negative attitude.*

Specialist

Characteristics
Specialists are dedicated individuals who pride themselves on acquiring technical skills and specialized knowledge. Their priorities focus on maintaining professional standards and on furthering and defending their own field. Eventually, the Specialist becomes the expert by sheer commitment along a narrow front.

As managers, they command support because they know more about their subject than anyone else and can usually be called upon to make decisions based on in-depth experience. While they show great pride in their own subject, they may lack interest in other people's subjects.

Role on a Team
Specialists have an indispensable part to play in some teams, for they provide the rare skill or knowledge that is key to fixing the problem being addressed.

A Specialist in action

Showing strengths
The site review council at a dialysis clinic is reviewing data on patient performance over the past months. The nurses are telling the team about problems that some patients are having with the traditional "ports" used to access arm veins for the dialysis treatment.

At that point, Lee pipes up: "I just saw a report in the latest nursing journals where they were testing a new device for accessing veins through the chest. I did more research and it appears this new device is legit. Maybe we should invite one of the reps here and see if it would work for those patients."

> COMMENT: *Specialists pride themselves in being expert in an area of their choosing. Though not always focused on the immediate needs, they must be allowed time to explore their discipline because someday that knowledge will come in handy.*

Showing a weakness

After a presentation by the company rep for the new device, Lee has become a strong advocate. When the rest of the team wants to proceed cautiously and even visit other clinics where the device is being used, she thinks that extra effort is a waste of time. "I know what I'm talking about here," she complains. "Why don't you trust me?"

> COMMENT: *Specialists tend to view the world through their narrow lens of expertise. They can sometimes get so enamored of what they're doing that they fail to see the larger picture.*

Shaper

Characteristics

Shapers are highly motivated people with a lot of nervous energy and a strong need for achievement. Usually, they are aggressive extroverts and possess strong drive. Shapers like to lead from the front and to push others into action. If obstacles arise, they will find a way around them. Headstrong and assertive, they tend to show strong emotional response to any form of disappointment or frustration.

Shapers generally make good managers because they generate action and thrive under pressure. Shapers are thick-skinned and argumentative and may lack interpersonal understanding. They are the most competitive team role, with a strong desire to win.

Role on a Team

They are probably the most effective members of a team in guaranteeing positive action. Shapers are excellent at sparking life into a team and are very useful in groups where political complications are apt to slow things down. As the name implies, they try to impose some shape or pattern (often their own) on group discussion or activities. Care must be taken to ensure their goals are aligned with those of the team as a whole.

A Shaper in action

Showing strengths

Bill leads the acquisition department in a financial services firm. He was becoming frustrated with his team. A new deal was in the works, but the advisory team couldn't seem to come to a decision. Norm was still manning the phones, surfacing alternative acquisition targets for the team to explore. Ellen was trying to map out the proposed acquisition in excruciating detail.

Bill stepped in to call a halt to all of the meandering. He knew the company had to grow or they would be gobbled up themselves. In the next two days after this intervention, Bill had lined up all the financing, gotten corporate approval, and was ready to take the plunge.

> COMMENT: *Shapers are fearless and action-oriented. Their energy can be just what some teams need.*

Showing a weakness

The acquisition looks like it's a go, but in the final meeting, Ellen kept raising practical issues for the team to explore. "Given the other three deals we have in the pipeline, I just want to make sure this is the best use of our resources," she says.

This is the last straw for Bill. "I'm really losing patience with this!," he yelled. "We have looked at this acquisition every which way from Sunday. Stop dinking around, Ellen. We would have this deal done by now if it weren't for you."

> COMMENT: *Shapers are often impatient, and can be abrasive since they don't fear controversy. It's allowable that they act this way, but that doesn't give them license to ride roughshod over others. In fact, in this case, Bill later apologized to Ellen and the rest of the team, explaining that his anxiety around getting the deal done had gotten the better of him. He acknowledged that Ellen had some good points around resource usage, and the team had some productive discussions on that issue.*

Implementer

Characteristics

Implementers have practical common sense and a good deal of self-control and discipline. They favor hard work and tackle problems in a systematic fashion. On a wider front the Implementer is typically a person whose loyalty and interests lie with the company and who is less concerned with the pursuit of self-interest. Implementers are useful to an organization because of their reliability and capacity for applied action.

Good Implementers often progress to high management positions by virtue of strong organizational skills and competency in tackling necessary tasks. They succeed because they are efficient and because they have a sense of what is feasible and relevant. However, they may lack spontaneity and show signs of rigidity.

Role on a Team

An Implementer will do what needs to be done. They are especially good at establishing project plans and anticipating barriers that need to be addressed. Once such plans are established, they may be reluctant to deviate from the set pathway.

An Implementer in action

Showing strengths

Maxwell Accounting Systems is considering the purchase of a major new contact management software. The CFO has already made the decision to go ahead with the purchase and is meeting with the head IT guy and Carlotta, who will be in charge of the conversion project. At the beginning of the meeting, Carlotta points out a potential roadblock to the others. "Did you realize that you set the purchase date just two months ahead of when we're moving the offices?" she asked. Juan, the CFO, chimed in. "I'm not clear why that's a problem. Two months is plenty of time to get the new system up and running, and it won't be affected by the move."

"You're right," answers Carlotta, "but I've seen the master moving plan and about half the people in every department are going to be tied up a good 6 to 8 weeks before the move—and those are the same people we need to support the software upgrade. I think it will overlap too much."

> COMMENT: *Implementers always have an eye on the practical aspects of any decision, "what will it take to make this work?"*

Showing a weakness

Juan, Carlotta, and the IT head honcho decided to move the purchase date for the new contact management program until two weeks after the big move. As they begin fleshing out the details of the changeover, it's clear that Carlotta is increasingly uncomfortable. "You know," she says, "we've been using Lotus Notes for about seven years now and it seems to work fine. Are you sure the change will help us?"

> COMMENT: *Implementers can be a little inflexible at times, preferring the comfort of the known to the uncertainty and risk of trying something new. Some reluctance is allowable, and the team just needs to be patient to make sure the Implementer understands the full logic and reasoning behind a decision. What becomes unallowable is when an Implementer gets so entrenched in their own comfort zone that they sabotage progress on important issues.*

Completer Finisher

Characteristics

Completer Finishers have a great capacity for follow-through and attention to detail. They are unlikely to start anything that they cannot finish. They are motivated by internal anxiety, yet outwardly they may appear unruffled. Typically, they are introverted and require little in the way of external stimulus or incentive. Completer Finishers can be intolerant of those with a casual disposition. They are not often keen on delegating, preferring to tackle all tasks themselves.

In management they excel by the high standards to which they aspire, and by their concern for precision, attention to detail and follow-through.

Role on a Team

Completer Finishers are invaluable where tasks demand close concentration and a high degree of accuracy. They foster a sense of urgency within a team and are good at meeting schedules.

A Completer Finisher in action

Showing strengths

The product design team couldn't survive without Peter. His attention to detail was famous companywide. He would test and re-test and test again each product feature. While this sometimes slowed down development, it was well known that any product he had touched would launch perfectly. Everybody wants Peter on their team because they know they can rely on him to get his assignments done completely.

> *COMMENT: Completer Finishers are essential to any team that actually wants to see results from its decisions. They are the people that will execute plans to the tiniest detail, meeting high standards of performance at every step.*

Showing a weakness

During the development of one product, new information came to light that affected the design of a feature that Peter was responsible for. The requested change really put him back. "But we've already tested everything and it works perfectly. We can't change things now. It would mess up everything." The team leader suggests that if Peter doesn't want to handle the change, perhaps someone else on the team could step in. "No way," says Peter. "This is my baby. I know how this works better than anyone else."

> *COMMENT: Some degree of perfectionism is not only expected but desirable in Completer Finishers. It's that attention to detail that everyone comes to rely on. But they can sometimes move towards obsession and can be very uncomfortable with change.*

Resource Investigators

Characteristics

Resource Investigators are often enthusiastic, extroverted, and quick to act. They are good at communicating with people both inside and outside the company. Although not necessarily a great source of original ideas, the Resource Investigator is effective when it comes to picking up other people's ideas and developing them. As the name suggests, they are skilled at finding out what is available and what can be done. Resource Investigators have relaxed personalities and are highly inquisitive. They are quick to see the possibilities in anything new and act opportunistically. Resource Investigators are commonly found in outward-looking positions such as sales and marketing.

Role on a Team

Resource Investigators are good at exploring and reporting back on ideas, developments or resources outside the team. They have an ability to think on their feet and to probe others for information. However, unless they remain stimulated by others, their enthusiasm rapidly fades.

A Resource Investigator in action

Showing strengths

The accounts payable team was really on the hot spot. Customer complaints about invoice and payment problems had been rising for months, and nothing they'd tried had worked. They'd upgraded their training, redesigned some software interface screens, but to little effect. Then one day Jamal came in very excited. "I was at a Rotary meeting last night and ran into Mark, one of the guys over at Maxwell Accounting. I was chatting with him about our low ratings and asked if he had any insights he could offer. He said our recent changes in product codes were causing lots of headaches at their end. Orders were getting messed up, which meant they had to ask for return authorizations and credit vouchers.

"On my way in this morning," continued Jamal, "I stopped by Derek's office and got his input on the code changes, then asked him to come talk to the whole team. I think we can brainstorm some ways to make our internal changes completely invisible to the customer."

> *COMMENT: Resource Investigators are the ultimate networkers. They just naturally foster connections with lots of people, and will use those connections to help identify solutions to problems, to draw in expertise when the team needs it. They are the people most likely to make sure that viewpoints from stakeholders outside the team are represented during discussions and decision making.*

Showing a weakness

When Jamal got back to his desk after the meeting with Derek and his team, he got a call from a colleague in another department. "Where's that report you promised me this morning?" asked the colleague. "It slipped my mind," confessed Jamal. "I got this great insight for solving this complaint problem we've been having and spent the morning working on that."

> *COMMENT: It's not unusual for Resource Investigators to forget some commitments when they get caught up in something that sparks their enthusiasm—especially when the latter requires them to talk to a lot of people. While this is allowable to some degree, the RI should find ways to get reminders about less-exciting commitments (like doing reports) so they don't let down customers or coworkers who may be depending on their work to make their own deadlines.*

Team Worker

Characteristics

Team Workers have a great capacity for flexibility and for adapting to different situations and people. They are perceptive and diplomatic. They are good listeners and are generally popular members of a group. They operate with sensitivity at work, but may be indecisive in crunch situations.

Team Workers are mild, sociable and concerned about others. It is not uncommon for Team Workers to become senior managers especially if divisional management is dominated by Shapers. This creates a climate in which their diplomatic and perceptive skills become real assets. As managers, they are seen as a threat to no one and therefore the most accepted and favored people to serve under.

Role on a Team

Team Workers have a lubricating effect on teams. Morale is better and people seem to cooperate better when they are around. Their role is to prevent interpersonal problems from arising within a team and thus allow all team members to contribute effectively. Not liking friction, they will go to great lengths to avoid it.

A Team Worker in action

Showing strengths

Gerry and Helen were really going at it. Gerry thought Helen was ignoring customer data by suggesting the team go with an option for using a cheaper material in the product design. Helen thought Gerry was being naïve about what the company could afford in product cost. Each was on the verge of stalking out of the meeting when Keith stepped in. "You know, I think you both have some good points here. Gerry's right that we have to be careful not to go with a cheaper material if it's going to harm the structural integrity. But Helen's right that we have very firm price targets for this product and our profit margins will be too low if we spend too much on materials. I think there's a way we could go with the more expensive material without harming potential profit margin ."

> COMMENT: As the name implies, Team Workers are inherently concerned that the team survive and work well as a unit. They will always be looking for ways to soothe over tense situations while making sure that all viewpoints are acknowledged.

Showing a weakness

Keith was glad that his suggestions for moving beyond the conflict between Helen and Gerry was accepted by the team. He clearly remembered a meeting not long ago when something similar happened, only this time Helen put him on the spot, asking him to choose sides between two alternatives suggested for the design of another element. He was extremely uncomfortable, not wanting to offend anyone's feelings, and hemmed and hawed until Helen gave up trying to make him take a stance.

> COMMENT: Team Workers can be uncomfortable with conflict or being placed in a position where they are expected to do something that could be perceived as "taking sides" (pitting one group against another). Obviously, that feeds into their strength in wanting to seek harmony, but it isn't allowable as a mechanism to avoid dealing with the source of the conflict. Doing so blocks progress because the issues go underground and are never addressed.

Coordinator

Characteristics

Coordinators are quick to spot individual talents and to use them in the pursuit of group objectives. Coordinators are well placed when put in charge of a team of people with diverse skills and personal characteristics. Their motto might well be "consultation with control" and they usually believe in tackling problems calmly. Mature, trusting and confident, they delegate readily. In some organizations, Coordinators are inclined to clash with Shapers due to their contrasting management styles.

Role on a Team

The distinguishing feature of Coordinators is the ability to cause others to work towards shared goals. While not necessarily the cleverest members of a team, they have a broad outlook and generally command respect.

A Coordinator in action

Showing strengths

The HR team at a small company had the potential to be fractious. One member had been with the company for 15 years and was happy with the way things were. Another member was new to the company and brimming with suggestions of ways to do things differently.

Oscar, the HR manager and team leader, knew it was his job to make sure everyone had a chance to contribute. He established a ground rule for the team that they would always be open to hearing new ideas, and that the team would always strive for consensus around major decisions. During meetings, he'd occasionally rein in the enthusiasm of the new guy, while at the same time making sure the most senior employee got her say. By maintaining an impartiality, he was able to steer the team towards effective decisions without appearing to take sides. He also kept on top of when the team would need other resources, such as experts in the various areas of benefits (healthcare, retirement plans, vacation, etc.), and always made sure that the right people were in the room together.

> COMMENT: *Coordinators are very skilled at building synergy on a team. They don't usually try to persuade people directly, but rather shape the meeting or discussion process so consensus emerges over time and people convince themselves of what the best options are. They are good at managing resources and coordinating actions so that handoffs between people work seamlessly.*

Showing a weakness

When it came time to draft a new retirement plan, Oscar let Tim, the new guy, take the lead, asking him to work with an external retirement plan specialist to develop a draft proposal for the whole team to review. He intended to check in with Tim a few times a week, but often got distracted by all other tasks. Then he got a call one day from the external specialist, "Listen, Oscar, you know I'm happy to help out, but I think Tim is asking me to make decisions that really you should be making. I think you'd be happier with the result if you were more involved at this stage."

> COMMENT: *Coordinators are often so busy coordinating that they can lose track of what's going on with the details of all their projects. It can reach a point where other team members may perceive them as abdicating responsibility, though that is rarely their intent. The Coordinator should help clarify expectations up front about their ongoing involvement and make sure others know they can call them in as necessary.*

Part II

Team Effectiveness

Introduction

You've been asked to serve on T.M.I.T.E. (pronounced "tee-mite"—The Most Ineffective Team Ever). At the first meeting, Mr. Magoo, the T.M.I.T.E. team leader, asks each team member to share their worst team stories, with the intent that these practices become the new norms for T.M.I.T.E.

LaToya is the first to speak up: "The first meeting for one project I was on was scheduled to start at 10 o'clock. I showed up on time and was the only person in the room. The team leader showed up ten minutes late. One guy was on the road and we were supposed to call him, but nobody had his number and there wasn't a speaker phone in the room. It went downhill from there."

"That's great," said Mr. Magoo. "I'd write that down on a flipchart, but then we'd have a record of what you said, so I won't.... Who wants to go next?"

Jack was the next to speak up. "At one team meeting I went to, this one guy passed around a twenty-page technical report with a lot of equations, gave us five minutes to skim it, then we had to make a decision right away. Nobody really knew what was going on."

"Wonderful," Mr. Magoo said. "I won't write that down, either. Anyone else?" He looked at Toni sitting at the back of the room. "How about you, young lady?"

"I don't really know why I'm here," said Toni.

"That's perfect," said Mr. Magoo. "Next?"

"Well," said a short guy sitting next to Mr. Magoo. "my last team kept going around and around and around without ever making any decisions. There were these two women who couldn't seem to agree on anything. And they wouldn't listen to anyone else. They'd just keep rehashing the same points over and over again. Then we'd run out of time in the meeting and have to start the mess all over again the next time around. We met every week for three months and had nothing to report."

"That sounds ideal for our purposes," commented Mr. Magoo. "I do so love the image of such unbalanced participation."

"I can top all of this," piped up Brenda. "I was on a team once that was told to start developing new products—something this company had never done before. We spent six months fleshing out a new product development process, figuring you had to have that in place before you could do any products. Our manager went ballistic when we presented the results. 'We wanted to launch a new product by the end of the year, and you guys have been messing about on a new process,' he yelled at us." "Six months effort, down the drain. The lost time alone must have cost the company a hundred thousand dollars or more."

Mr. Magoo smiled. "This is all terrific. I'm so pleased. And what do you have to offer?" he added, looking directly at YOU...

We all have horror stories from teams that were run badly, meetings that were a complete waste of time, projects that failed miserably. In this section of the book, we look at what goes into creating a much rosier picture: a team that really hums, does good work, produces great results, and feels good about its accomplishments. There are a lot of essential practices that fall under this topic, but we'll focus on three areas that are most critical to getting off to a good start:

1) Getting alignment within the team and with sponsors (Chapter 3)

2) Creating processes for working together effectively (Chapter 4)

3) Being clear about responsibilities and assignments (Chapter 5)

CHAPTER 3

Creating Alignment
Around Shared Goals

Six weeks ago, Tim and his process improvement team were given the goal to "raise revenues by 5%." At first, they thought that sounded clear enough. But they are a Six Sigma team that is supposed to use the DMAIC methodology to do process improvement. They have been struggling in the Define phase ever since, fighting over which process to map (some wanted to look at sales, others marketing, and a few thought improving customer service had that kind of potential).

Various team members had talked to people in sales, marketing, and customer services to get their perspectives on what the problem was, but no clear patterns emerged. Tensions were running high on the team, and everyone was frustrated with the lack of progress.

Out of desperation and a desire to get things moving, Tim called for a tollgate review to assess progress and get the project through to the next phase, Measure.

The meeting did not go well. Their presentations were harshly questioned by the project sponsor, who felt that they were going in circles. After a good deal of debate in a tollgate review that ran

twice as long as anticipated, the management
team at the site decided to kill the project.

The first and most important challenge that faces every team—and what Tim's team failed to do—is gaining a shared understanding of team goals and making sure their understanding matches what the team sponsor or champion expects. In Tim's case, there was a lot of blame to go around. Their sponsor had given them a poorly defined goal, and the team hadn't worked to pin down what exactly they were supposed to do before plunging into the project.

Often the process of gaining alignment is given short shrift, overlooked, or taken for granted. We routinely see that newly formed teams with a task in front of them dive directly into action with very little discussion of why that action is important or in fact what it is that the team hopes to accomplish. This tendency is exacerbated by the time pressures all too common in the workplace.

Unfortunately, the long-term consequences of this bias towards action doom many teams, initiatives, and companies to failure:

- If members have different interpretations, the team will spend endless unproductive hours in debate over priorities, necessary actions, and optimal solutions
- If the team does not understand what management wants (which should reflect business priorities), or if the project sponsor doesn't understand how the team is interpreting its mission, several things could happen (none of which are desirable):
  - The team could invest months of time and effort

solving the wrong problem—and therefore be seen as a failure by all the bosses
- The sponsor may not support the team as actively as needed because he or she doesn't see the effort as a priority

One tool used by many teams and their sponsors to gain alignment is a **project charter**, a document that authorizes the formation of a team and sets forth its purpose. Such a document is certainly helpful to a team, but it's the discussions that go on as part of the charter development that really add value. In this chapter, we'll walk through how to develop a charter and how to make sure you have alignment around the team's purpose.

Developing a charter is handled in different ways by different managers. In our experience, it's best if the project sponsor drafts most or all of the charter and then gives it to the Green Belt or Black Belt and their team to execute. This division of labor ensures that the goals set forth within the charter itself reflect the true business requirements as seen by the project sponsor.

However, in some situations a sponsor may give the team only a general direction and ask the team leader to prepare a draft charter for review based on research the team does to better define the issue. In practice, this approach has proven risky because it's seldom accompanied by a check *back* with the sponsor—so it's not uncommon to find that when the Green Belt or Black Belt writes the charter, a team ends up working on a problem that is not important to the business leader(s). This misalignment almost ensures the failure of the project at some point down the road.

In case you're ever called on to write a charter yourself, we'll walk through all the elements and their purpose. Even if you're only given a draft charter, this information will help you understand what your sponsor was trying to accomplish and help you frame better questions for clarification to take back to your sponsor.

Belbin differences exacerbate misalignment

The natural tendencies we all exhibit as captured in our Belbin profiles are fuel for unproductive conflict on a team that has no clear charter. The Shapers will get impatient with the Plants and Resource Investigators who are having a great time exploring every possible angle they can spin on the goal. Coordinators will be run ragged trying to keep track of everything that's going on. Team Workers may blow a few circuits trying to get agreement among a team that's going off in every direction. Specialists may either become over-bearing or drop into the background depending on whether some the many directions the team takes fall inside or outside their area of expertise.

In short, what can result is pure chaos on a team. In contrast, a team where every member understands and agrees on its purpose can much better focus Belbin strengths in a positive direction.

Writing a Useful Charter

Good project charters should be fairly concise (one to two pages), but still describe a project in sufficient detail that other executives within the business understand what is being undertaken. A basic project charter has six elements in the following order:

1 Business Impact—what benefits a successful project will bring to the business

2 Problem Statement - what pain is being felt currently within the business

3 Goal Statement - what the future state will look like

4 Project Scope - what will be addressed by the project and what will be excluded from consideration

5 Team Composition - who will be on the core project team

6 Project Timing - how long the project will take and any major milestones and forecasted completion dates

This sequence is based on what the average reader of the charter is most interested in: what the business benefits of the project will be. In fact, this is one of the main functions of project charters—they serve as a summary of all projects being considered for launch. On a periodic basis, senior executives will meet to determine which projects will be launched. They will base their decisions primarily on the contents of all the charters in front of them; poor or inaccurate charters will lead to poor prioritization decisions by the management team. Similarly, flaws in the charter will ultimately force the team down unproductive paths during their initial time together, and it is quite common for the team to have to stop entirely and start over if the charter is vague, unclear, or misinterpreted.

In comparison to the sequence of charter elements above, the development process is sequentially a little bit different.

Here's how it usually works:

1. Write the Problem Statement

The problem statement is in its simplest form a description of the current state and the pain being felt right now. It should characterize the problem in about one paragraph by answering the following questions:

    a) WHAT is happening?

    b) WHERE is it occurring?

    c) WHEN does it occur? –or- WHEN did the problem start?

    d) What is the EXTENT of the problem?

Take care to ensure that the answers to these questions are only describing the current state. One common pitfall is to let a solution or desired future state creep into the problem statement—what you *want* to have happen is information that belongs in the goal statement (or should be removed entirely). Another pitfall in this section is when people include assumptions as to the cause of the problem. Note that the WHY question is nowhere to be found above. It will be the role of the team to determine the root cause of why the problem exists and to devise solutions which address those fundamental causes.

The best problem statements also contain a good deal of data, not just anecdotal statements. The data or estimates serve to help convey the problem more accurately to the readers of the charter. If some data is missing or needs to be verified, including it in the problem statement is fine as long as it is highlighted as being an assumption to be verified later. One common practice is to underline any data of this sort or to include a "TBD" statement after it. Examples of good and bad problem statements are shown in Table 3.A:

Table 3.A: Providing Details in Problem Statements

Bad	Good
Our customers complain about our machine maintenance service all the time. The repair technicians' morale is getting lower all the time.	Response time for equipment repair and maintenance in the Northeast region is much slower (avg. = 7 hrs) than what we promise customers (4 hrs). The longest delays appear to be on Monday each week, but do occur sporadically all week. Several customers (representing over 30% of last years sales) have threatened to buy their next machines from our competition.
The sales force is tired of spending their time on billing issues instead of sales calls.	In the third quarter, the average sales rep in North America spends over 15 hours per week with customers on billing discrepancies. They estimate that over 30% (TBD) of invoices contain one or more errors. This results in dissatisfied existing customers and fewer sales calls to potential new customers. The problem seems to be getting worse each quarter.

2. Map the problem to the underlying process

In the next step, the problem(s) should be linked to some repetitive process. This is a key step often overlooked by managers and executives. It is much more common for them to see the world or their business as a series of one-time events ("That customer got upset because we gave them the wrong pricing"), rather than the problems being indicative of a broken process ("Our pricing process is too complex, which results in the potential for errors when communicating with our customers"). The reason this step is critical can be seen in what the team is tasked to do: process improvement (not problem elimination). Without a process to study, they will struggle mightily as they apply a methodology like Lean or Six Sigma.

If you don't have an existing label for the process associated with the problem, create a "process name" in the form of an action verb and an object ("dispatching a repair technician" or "creating an invoice"). It is essential that the process name imply or correlate to a repetitive process (many technicians are dispatched each day, and many invoices get created every month). The final check is to make sure that the problem(s) described in the problem statement appear to be caused by the process just named in this step.

3. Create a SIPOC chart

A SIPOC chart is one of the easiest and most powerful process analysis tools within the Lean Six Sigma toolkit.

SIPOC is an abbreviation of SUPPLIER-INPUT-PROCESS-OUTPUT-CUSTOMER. It explodes the process under study into a graphical representation of material and/or information flow, the resources required and how the process can be measured. These items will form the basis for the next three sections of the project charter itself: goal statement, project scope, and business impact.

In developing a SIPOC chart (see template below), the chart is worked backwards from the customer back to the supplier. The following sequence of events should occur:

a) Name the process (step 2 above)

b) Brainstorm who the CUSTOMER(s) of the process are. This can be anyone who gets something from the process (a good or service, a report, a request or notification, etc.)

c) For each customer, determine what they get from the process. These OUTPUTS are usually a "thing"—a tangible object or a set of information.

d) Determine what steps are needed to provide the output. That is the PROCESS steps. A good rule of thumb is to divide the process into about five steps. Give them names that start with a verb.

e) Now consider what INPUTS are required for the process to work properly and generate the outputs. Hint: think about what things (material, information) are consumed or used up when people do their work. This will help you differentiate between resources like labor, which is part of the process, from the inputs that are changed into outputs.

f) For each input, determine where it comes from; this is the SUPPLIER. Suppliers are persons, businesses, or departments.

g) Lastly, brainstorm how you could measure the quality
of process for each element—what would tell you if an
input met specifications? If a process steps was being
done correctly? If the output met customer needs?
Think in terms of speed, quality or accuracy, and
cost.Do not confine yourself to measurements you
already have in place. (See examples at the bottom of
Figure 3.1)

Completing a SIPOC forces people to view the problem in
a systemic manner. In our experience, the worst charters are
the ones written without having performed a SIPOC. The
next three sections of the charter will make extensive use of
the SIPOC.

Figure 3.1: SIPOC Example

*S*upplier	*I*nput	*Process*	*O*utput	*C*ustomer

Creating an Invoice

Supplier	Input	Process	Output	Customer
Sales Reps	Acct. Activity	Get Acct. Activity	Monthly Invoice	Client
		Get Customer Info		
Marketing	Base Plans	Apply Pricing		Accounts Receivable
	Pricing Table	Calculate Totals		
Mail Room	Blank Forms	Print Invoice		
	Stamps	Mail Invoice		

Input Measures
• # of price points
• # of transactions
• # of service items
• % accuracy of info

Process Measures
• % of info missing
• # follow -up phone
  calls to sales reps
• # unprintable invoices
• % accountants trained
• # items per invoice

Output Measures
• % of invoices correct
• # of errors
• # of invoices
• Time required (days)

4. Write the Goal Statement

The goal statement is intended to describe the desired future state which will exist once the project is successfully completed. It is imperative that the goal statement be written based on what the new value of one or more of the outputs will be. In our example diagrammed in the SIPOC, the most important of the measures might be the percentage of invoices which are completely correct. The goal of the project might be to "improve this rate from the current 70% to 95%" (customers would like that number to reach 100% eventually, but an initial gain of 25 percentage points is significant and may be all that's practical immediately).

Which output measure the sponsor chooses to focus on will have major implications for the conduct of the team. If the focus was the amount of time required to produce invoices rather than invoice accuracy, the entire project would be different. The team would be forced to look at the labor efficiency and delays within the invoicing process, rather than where the errors are being injected into the invoices. As you can also see, both of these output measures pertain to the same output: an invoice. This is why it is so critical to lock in on the output measures rather than the output "things."

In some companies which emphasize statistical process improvement methods, another part of the goal statement is a $Y = f(X)$ equation which lists all of the possible contributing causes of the problem. This approach, if used, should focus only on the measures —the Y is the output measure and the Xs are the input and process measures. All of the measures can be pulled from the completed SIPOC.

We'll go into more detail about goal statements and checking for alignment around the goals later in this chapter.

5. Determine the Project Scope

The project scope statements are usually comprised of two components: what is in scope and what is out of scope. The "Out of Scope" portion is often the most significant. It will be used by the team to prevent any form of scope creep later on in the project. Things that may be deemed out of scope include: some of the process steps, certain customers or products, one location or part of the organization, some potential solutions like those requiring new equipment, etc.

Determining the proper scope can be aided by the SIPOC as well. Once the output measure and target level have been decided on, it is usually possible to speculate on where the project should look for root causes (certain sub-process steps or some of the inputs). It will be up to the team to ultimately prove the root cause relationships, but it may become apparent that some areas can be safely ruled as "out of scope."

6. Calculate the Business Impact

The Business Impact statement is merely the "dollar-ization" of closing the gap between current state and desired future state. It is founded upon the goal statement and what monetary (or other) benefits will result once the things being measured move from their current values to the targets set out in the goal statement (for example, how much will the company gain by cutting cycle time in half). It is critical that any assumptions behind the calculation are made explicit and that data that needs further validation be highlighted as well. The calculations themselves should be laid out algebraically so that the logic and causality is apparent to the reader of the charter.

In the invoicing example in the SIPOC diagram, the business impact will be based on moving the rate of correct invoices mailed to clients from 70% to 95%.

7. Select a Project Team

For the purposes of project prioritization, it may be sufficient to merely identify what types of resources will be required to be present on the team (someone from finance, one or two accountants, a sales rep, etc.). As a general rule, the scope of the project will help guide what type of skills or knowledge need to be represented within the core team members. Once the decision is made to launch the project, one of the first activities will be to finalize the membership of the team. The importance of diversity, either in viewpoint of knowledge or in terms of Belbin Team Role balance, should be a primary consideration. Generally, the project sponsor and Black Belt or Green Belt work jointly on determining who will be on the team.

8. Estimate Project Timing

Project timing is often the hardest thing to estimate on the charter. As a guideline, Black Belt DMAIC projects will generally take from 13 to 20 weeks, depending on a variety of factors (the experience of the Black Belt, scope of the project, complexity of the process under study, how much data is already being measured, etc.). It is often wise to involve someone with a great deal of experience with similar projects in the development of the initial timelines.

Regardless of what the overall duration of the project is determined to be, the next step will be the estimation of when the first few milestones can be reached. These should be included in the Project Timing discussion and used to pace the team through the initial phases of the project.

Figure 3.2: Example Charter

Sample Project Charter

Business Impact

This project will increase the amount of time sales reps spend selling by reducing the time they spend on correcting billing and invoicing errors.

Time Savings = 50 hrs/wk X (30% now - 5% future) = 12.5 hrs/wk per sales rep

Extra Sales Calls = 12.5 hrs/wk ÷ 5 hrs/call X 50 wks/yr. X 40 reps = 5,000 calls

Revenue = 5,000 calls X 20% win rate X $10,000 avg. sale = $10,000,000

Profits = $10,000,000 X 30% gross margin = $3,000,000 pre-tax

Figure 3.2, cont.

Problem Statement
In the third quarter, the average sales rep in North America spends over 15 hours per week with customers on billing discrepancies. They estimate that over 30% (TBD) of invoices contain one or more errors. This results in dissatisfied existing customers and fewer sales calls to potential new customers. The problem seems to be getting worse each quarter.

Goal Statement
The goal of this project is to reduce the number of incorrect invoices sent to the customer, from the current rate of 30% to 5%.
Our initial hypothesis is that most of the errors today are the result of incorrect information supplied by the sales reps and customer service specialists during the initial submission of customer information.

Project Scope
Out of Scope = pricing plans, accounts receivable and collections
In Scope = North America only

Project Team
Black Belt from N.Am. Sales
1-2 sales reps
2-3 accountants from billing department
1 regional controller

Project Timing
Assuming a launch date of January 1, 2006:
Define Tollgate @ Jan 21
Measure Tollgate @ Feb 15
Project complete by the end of April

Aligning Around Goals

Goal setting has been the focus of numerous studies for both individual and team performance. The findings are largely the same in both cases: In one study, it was determined that over 70% of teams who set explicit, clear goals achieve those goals. This is remarkable in that other surveys of team-based initiatives routinely report that far less than 50% of teams are successful in achieving their stated objectives in the time given. The power of goal setting, whether it be for a team or at the individual level, is demonstrated by a study of alumni at a major U.S. university. It was determined that while enrolled only 3% of the alumni set personal goals each year. A survey 20 years later revealed that the combined net worth of this 3% exceeded the combined total net worth of the 97% who had not set personal goals.

Concrete, tangible goals are crucial to ensuring that the goals are universally understood within the team and that there is no room for rationalizations to creep into a poorly performing team. The team needs to be able to see its performance in very concrete terms in a simple yes/no fashion; shades of gray only serve to let energy and motivation evaporate. Good goals are:

- Concrete and tangible: Goals that can be experienced or observed through the five senses—this makes them real
- Measurable: Having numerical targets ensures that the planning to follow is aligned with what the goal truly is, which allows the team to better evaluate alternative solutions and gauge progress

- Time-bounded: This ensures that the team is conserving a precious resource and helps maintain a sense of urgency towards goal achievement
- Written down: Documented and publicly displayed to have maximum effect. Having a goal hanging on the wall during team meetings is a not-so-subtle reminder of why the team exists and what the outcomes must be to be considered successful.

Examples of typical goal statements and how they can be improved are shown in Table 3.B.

Table 3.B: Improving Goal Statements

Criteria	Poor	Good
Concrete & Tangible	"Get better at golf"	"Shoot a lower score"
Measurable	"Score better"	"Shoot 90 or lower in 75% of my rounds"
Time Bounded	"when I get around to it"	By August 15th
Documented	Unexpressed, not even discussed with another person	Written on the bag tag and the bathroom mirror

The importance of stretch in the goal

Setting the goal at the correct level is also of critical concern. Teams will work diligently towards their goal but once it is reached often tend to lose focus or motivation. In one classic experiment, teams of four people were tasked to stack as many matchboxes as possible in a tower before the tower crumbled. The rules of the game were that only one person could touch the match boxes and that person would be blindfolded. The other three people could only coach the stacker verbally. The three coaches were told to leave the room and agree on their estimate of the maximum height that could be reached; their estimate was not revealed to the stacker. They were then readmitted to the room, and the stacking commenced.

Two very interesting things occurred among the many teams playing this game. First, teams who set higher goals actually created higher stacks of matchboxes. While some teams failed to reach their stretch goals, there was a strong correlation between actual results and what the goal was. Secondly, it was noted that of the teams that reached their goals, few significantly outperformed them. It was rare that a team would outperform their goal by more than one or two matchboxes; this was true even of teams that set very conservative goals. For whatever reasons, the target levels agreed on became self-fulfilling prophecies for the team of coaches. Interest and involvement were high as long as their was a gap between current state and desired future, but as soon as the goal was reached, the teams tended to wander and become largely indifferent to the task at hand.

Checking for shared goals

Making sure that everyone on a team has a shared understanding of its goals is the first step to developing trust within the team; as progress is made towards the team goals the contributions of each team member are valued in this context by the other members. It also positions the team as a unique entity, independent of the team members themselves. Team members gain the ability to challenge a course of action as being inconsistent with the stated and agreed goals of the team. This will help the team stay focused, avoid tangents, and resist the tendency to expand the scope of the project as it progresses.

The mechanisms for setting joint goals can be challenging, but the overall impact is clearly evident. The first benefit is that the team creates a jointly shared vision of what is to be accomplished. If the mechanisms are implemented effectively, commitment from the team is generated versus mere compliance.

In our experience, the best methods for developing shared goals have one unique characteristic: **individual team members write down their interpretation of the goal prior to any joint discussion**. This levels the playing field and gives the team a much broader set of alternatives to consider. If a free-form discussion occurs without preparation, two pitfalls commonly occur: the most senior person in the room carries the day and/or the first idea expressed is given undue weight (essentially, it must be disproven before other options are considered). Finally, the individual preparation prior to joint discussion clarifies each individual's thinking about what they want from the team.

Taking the time to do this alignment makes achieving the goals more personally meaningful to each team member.

This is one way to structure the goals discussion for a project team:

- The team leader shares whatever information has been passed down from the project sponsor or management
- Individuals write down their interpretation of what the goal should be
- The team discusses all of the differing options and reaches joint agreement on one final version of the goal

Do a WIIFM & Concerns checks, too

While you're doing a check on how team members interpret the tangible goal given to the team, take the time to explore the personal aspect of participation in the project. There are two aspects to this "What's In It For Me" (WIIFM) discussion:

1) How achieving the team goal will affect the team members personally ("I won't have to take any more complaint calls from customers" or "I'll be able to get twice as much done in a day").

2) What personal goals people are bringing to the project. For example, someone may be interested in getting more experience in collecting and analyzing data, someone else in doing customer interviews, and another in honing their writing and documentation skills. Sharing these personal goals with the team

would help ensure that people are given the opportunity when the time comes.

The flipside of what people hope to gain from the project is the personal concerns they may have about participation. Hearing these concerns is equally important so the team can plan accordingly.

For example, consider the harm it could do if a team member under considerable time pressure did not disclose that fact upfront to the team. Weeks or months down the line, fellow team members may be frustrated with this person because of their lack of participation. (Put another way, a personal goal of this time-pressured person is to put the barest minimum of time into the project; meanwhile the goal of the rest of the team is to do the work thoroughly so they can achieve all their goals and look good to their bosses.)

Be forewarned: even when asked, people may be reluctant to share their concerns, especially if they think it will make them look bad to the team. It may be helpful to raise some issues with people in private. ("Vic, I know you're working on three other projects now. Do you think it's going to be a problem finding time to work on this one, too?" or "Jane, as I recall, you missed the training on interviews last month when you were out sick. Would it help if I went over the basics with you before our next meeting?")

One last note. It may be that some of the goals or concerns are beyond your ability to influence or solve. In that case, seek help from a Black Belt, project sponsor, champion, expert facilitator, etc.

Alignment with business goals

Many, many Green Belts and Black Belts attribute their success in a large measuring to having good support from their project sponsor or manager. The value of good support can't be overstated:

- With it, the team will get help eliminating barriers, finding resources, and making links to other parts of the company. They can be assured that the sponsor will continue working to maintain the results of the project.
- Without it, the team is likely dead in the water.

You must ask yourself what will increase the odds that your sponsor will actively support your team. The key to ensuring support comes back to WIIFM. If the sponsor sees the importance of the project to meeting their own business objectives (such as annual targets for their work unit), they will support the project and the team. Another key is to ensure that the sponsor also understands what the team is trying to do and agrees with how they intend to do it.

Alignment is not a one-time thing

Having probing discussions about purpose and direction up front is clearly a mandate for effective teams. But you can't stop at that. Throughout the project, team members will be uncovering information that further shapes their understanding of the issues at hand and possible solutions.

The tollgate reviews built into the DMAIC method are one way to ensure that this information is shared with project sponsors and that both the sponsor and team continue to agree on project direction, purpose, and scope. You may want to do more frequent checks with your sponsor, keeping him/her updated on what the team is learning and what that means for your direction. That way the sponsor has the opportunity to make course corrections before you've gone too far down a path he or she sees as unproductive or counter to business goals.

Conclusion

During a quick meeting with his project sponsor, Mark learned that he was to lead a new team whose goal was to "improve customer satisfaction with post-sales service to at least 90% with a collateral goal of increasing revenues from these customers by 10%"

Mark shared this goal and other charter information during a formal project team launch. The team members asked quite a few questions about the goal, which Mark took back to the spon-

sor. The conversations helped clarify the timeline (six months) and boundaries of the project (anything within customer service was fair game; they were not to address customer expectations raised by marketing or promotional materials, though questions of this nature should be passed back to the sponsor).

With those questions answered, the team plunged into its design work. Two weeks later the team notified the project sponsor that they were ready to hold the first tollgate meeting.

At the tollgate meeting, the team was able to present a detailed process map of a core customer service process. They also had done a great deal of work collecting customer requirements, some of which were very surprising to both the team and the managers at the tollgate. (Two of the findings led to "quick hit" improvements in how customer service reps answered common questions, which preliminary post-call surveys showed had bumped up customers satisfaction scores by 10 points.)

Furthermore, the team had been able to substantiate the business case for the project by validating some of the initial charter assumptions and tightening up the estimates of potential revenue increases. The team also presented their plans for the Measure phase. The project sponsor gave his approval to proceed into Measure; the team was one week ahead of their initial schedule.

The keys to Mark's early project success? He had been given a great project charter and had been able to get alignment between the sponsor and the team on the direction the project should take.

The common sense of this chapter is irrefutable: If you spend time identifying where you want to go and how you're going to get there, you stand a much better chance of reaching your goals. And when it comes to working on a team, that "you" has a plural meaning: the team *as a group* must agree on the goal and direction. The carcasses of many failed teams shows what happens if you just assume everyone is rowing in the same direction.

Developing a clear charter and gaining alignment are not rocket science, nor are they especially time consuming. The burden, such as it is, of taking these steps is minimal compared to what you'll gain in efficiency down the road.

CHAPTER 4

Planning Your Team Processes

Throughout the history of business, we're sure there have been teams that were run informally or without robust structures but still achieved or surpassed their goals. But once you've worked on and gotten used to how top teams operate with pit-crew-like efficiency, you will never want to go back to the old way of doing things haphazardly. Great teams develop structures which allow them to reach their goals and do it quickly. Efficient teams routinely do five things:

1. Run tight meetings
2. Use ground rules
3. Plan
4. Document and display progress
5. Use feedback

While these practices seem simple (and actually are), they are rarely routine practice within most large organizations. Teams that do not consistently perform these basic tasks suffer from inconsistent results. Worse still, team members often begrudge the time spent in meetings or team activities and eventually become reluctant to participate at all.

1. Run tight meetings

Imagine going into a meeting room and knowing exactly why you're there, having all your prep work done because you knew what information would be needed during the meeting, understanding what the group in the room is supposed to accomplish, and knowing the odds of getting in and out of the meeting quickly are definitely in your favor. That would be nice, wouldn't it? Four things you need to do to achieve that level of meeting performance are:

a) Come prepared

b) Use agendas

c) Manage the meeting time

d) Assign meeting responsibilities

a) Come prepared

The ability of a team to achieve its goals *during* its time together is greatly enhanced by making sure participants know specifically what prework they must perform *before* the meeting. In most meetings, teams spend a great deal of time in "level setting" or ensuring that all participants are aware of all the known facts or issues. Because these things are really one-way communication ("I know something and need to tell you about it"), they do not need to be part of the joint meeting time itself. Doing the information-sharing prior to the meeting therefore allows the team to use meeting time more wisely.

The best items to include in a prework package are those that are unambiguous or unlikely to require a great deal of explanation; they are easy to read and understand correctly. Typically, this includes minutes from the last meeting, agendas, standardized reports, and prepared background information. Avoid things like reams of raw data, controversial memos, random thoughts or hypotheses, or anything else that could easily be misinterpreted in written form.

Another great prework technique is to send out a "straw model" of a solution and ask people to examine, consider, and/or critique it individually prior to the meeting. A similar effect can be achieved by sending out a question to the meeting participants that they are to answer prior to the meeting. Requests for data also make good prework (everyone should collect and bring any available data which relates to Topic X).

It is imperative that the prework be sent out well in advance of the meeting. Failure to do this will result in some people arriving without having completed the prework, which defeats the whole intent in the first place. The amount of prework sent out and the time team members have available ultimately determine the notice required. One common rule of thumb employed by many teams is a minimum notice of two business days; another is that each additional hour to be spent on prework activities requires an additional two days' of notice. Both of these rules set a ratio of roughly one hour of prework to two day's notice, which should allow sufficient freedom to the team members to reallocate their time and complete the assignments.

One final benefit to employing prework for meetings is that it gives some control of the communication to the team members individually. Instead of being forced to spend the first hour of a 3-hour team meeting hearing about background information (which they may or not already know), they can review the prework when it best fits their schedule. They could also decide whether or not there was new information in the prework package and adjust the amount of time they need to devote to the prework. Neither of these choices is available when meeting time is used for one-way communication. Prework may not shorten an individual's overall time commitment to a team, but it gives them a bit more control over when their time must be invested (one hour at my discretion and only two hours in the meeting itself).

b) Use agendas

An agenda is a plan for how time in a meeting will be spent. Having a plan is essential to working efficiently. Without a plan, the team won't know what prework to assign (see previous topic) and will be less likely to manage its time wisely during the meeting.

All agendas should include the following information:
- Meeting start time
- Meeting end time
- Location of the meeting
- Main purpose of the meeting
- Topic heading(s)
- A brief description of each topic or heading

- Expected duration of each topic or phase of the meeting
- Who will be presenting or leading each topic

Figure 4.1: Sample agenda

Time:	*8:00am – 10:00am EST*
Date:	*Jan. 13, 2006*
Location:	*Conf. Rm. 207, 4 th Floor, Clark Building*
Purpose:	*Process mappping*

Agenda Item	Leader	Time
• Review prework	Steve	5 min
• Review agenda and goals	Steve	5 min
• Consolidate revisions to invoicing process maps (from prework)	Pam	50 min
• Add data on quality & accuracy	Tim	15 min
• Create "strawmodel" of map for the customer complaint process	Georgia	30 min
• Next Steps	Steve	10 min
• Benefits and Concerns	Steve	5 min

The purpose of an agenda is to provide a framework for meeting specific goals the team has identified—a decision about something, the development of a plan, some other concrete deliverable, etc. That's why in practice an agenda for one meeting is usually developed at the end of the previous meeting ("what do we need to accomplish next time? what agenda items should we include to do that?"). By starting from the outcome or deliverable, it will be much easier to stay focused during the meeting itself.

Once you have the outcomes and steps identified, allocate time (see next discussion) and identify who will be leading the discussion for each topic. Compile these notes, type up the agenda, and email or post it electronically well in advance of the meeting itself. (Worst case, if you don't get the agenda set ahead of time, make completing an agenda the first item of business during the meeting itself).

Allocating meeting time on the agenda

How to can you come up with reasonable time estimates? That's something you and the team will get better at with experience. To get started, it may help to divide long or complex topics into their components. A decision process, for example, will likely involve data sharing, data analysis, conclusions, solution generation, selection of a final solution, and next steps for implementation. Once you have that picture in mind, you will likely be able to estimate the time required more easily.

It's usually better to start this allocation process from the bottom-up, by estimating independently what each sub-process step will require, rather than starting top-down with the total time available and divvying up the minutes amongst items. (The bottom-up approach will tell you if your meeting needs to be longer or shorter than planned.)

Good teams always incorporate some flexibility into the allocation or enforcement of time buckets. Their estimates of the time required often end up as ranges rather than point estimates (20–30 minutes vs. 25 minutes).

Another key success factor in these teams is their inclusion of **buffer time** in one form or another: they may explicitly list 5% –10% of the time as "slack" or "buffer," or their estimates of time required may be set towards the upper end of the anticipated range. The underlying rationale for this flexibility and extra timing lies in the fact that team discussions are not deterministic; no one can predict accurately at the outset of a free-form discussion what will occur. When too much structure is applied to time management in such a forum, the quality of the discussions, interactions and ultimately decision-making all suffer.

Tip: Keep your meetings (and project) focused

One common pitfall in meetings is putting: too many topics for the time available. Meeting planners tend to to acquiesce to the demands of participants to "get it all done while we are together." This morphs a focused meeting into a series of related discussions. Unfortunately, rarely is any time added to the length of the meeting to accommodate the new topics. Meetings like this are rarely satisfying for the participants, nor do they produce stellar results.

In addition, it's more difficult to understand what did or did not go well with an unfocused meeting—there are simply too many variables to identify root causes of failure. Focused meetings are much easier to diagnose both for good ("what went well") and bad ("what didn't go well"). You can more easily point a finger at a specific element of the process (too little time, bad planning, failure to hear from everyone, etc.)—and therefore it is easier to determine corrective actions to use in the future.

c) Manage meeting time

Time is a scarce and ever-dwindling resource; it must be actively managed if you want to use it wisely. Doing time estimates for the agenda is the first step. The next step is to establish milestones at key intervals for longer items or the meeting as a whole and perform a status check to see where the team is in relation to the initial timing estimates they created.

Remember, the purpose of creating estimates isn't to get perfect at estimating, it's to allow intelligent use of time during a meeting. When one agenda item runs over, for example, the team will know that its plan needs to be adjusted: "We've used up the half-hour on our customer plan but still have a long way to go. Do we want to continue today and shift some later agenda items to the next meeting, or should we wrap this up, make assignments for the next meeting, and continue with the agenda?"

The key is to force the team to make deliberate choices about how its time is spent, rather than allow discussions to ramble on far past the point of diminishing returns.

d. Assign meeting responsibilities

If you've participated in any team sports, you know the teams work best when each person on a team has a specific job or role. Otherwise you end up like a peewee hockey team, with everybody trying to get to the puck all at the same time and no one minding the net!

Broader assignments

Chapter 5 will talk about assigning team responsibilities in a broader sense. Here, we're focused on what's needed to run a meeting effectively.

The most useful team positions in terms of meeting effectiveness are:

1. **Facilitator:** responsible for making sure that discussions are productive, that everyone has a chance to contribute, and that all of the possible data and knowledge is surfaced. The facilitator needs some knowledge of group discussion and decision techniques and ideally has some experience with navigating through conflict. In most cases, someone on the team can fill this role (even if they are "learning as you go"), though if you expect to tackle controversial or highly emotional issues, it helps to bring in an expert facilitator who is not part of the team.

Team leader AND facilitator?

Many teams find it helpful to separate the facilitation role from the team leader role. This prevents a concentration of power in one individual which can lead to a destructive steering effect, or bringing the team too quickly into alignment with the personal wishes of the team leader. The team leader role is typically given to the senior ranking member of the team or the project's sponsor or champion. To the extent that a tie-breaker role is required, it often is assigned to the team leader.

2. **Scribe:** responsible for ensuring that information which comes to light during discussion is both captured and made visible to the team. The simple act of capturing key points on a flipchart can ensures that a common understanding is formed within the team. It eliminates time wasted in later sorting out misunderstandings about previously agreed to points. By making the documentation visible, it is also possible to ensure that the true meaning or data is accurately reflected in the team records. Note that we have advocated the use of flipcharts rather than computers. In our experience the efficiency of a laptop-based note-taker is overshadowed by them or others being distracted by typing and not fully participating. Also, the data in a laptop tends to be visible only to one person, whereas flipcharts or whiteboards are visible to all.

3. **Process monitor:** responsible for whether the team is complying with the process or agenda they set forth initially. If not, the process monitor is empowered to call a timeout to discuss and re-establish the initial process or suggest that any contingency plans be invoked.

The overall goal of assigning specific meeting roles is to allow the team to operate more fluidly when they meet together. Care must be taken to ensure that an individual's assigned role does not impede their ability to participate in the discussions. Limiting what gets documented by the scribe will help in this regard. The facilitator, in particular, can suffer from the conflict between their role and personally participating. In cases where a conflict between participation and performance of a role exists, the team should either re-assign the role or perhaps consider splitting the role among two people. In extreme cases, it may be desirable to bring in an outside facilitator (another Black Belt or Green Belt, perhaps), so that everyone on the team can participate fully and equally in a discussion.

The assignment of roles should be made in accordance with the team's goals. A team with results-based goals will most likely attempt to assign roles to team members with demonstrated skill in performing those roles. Another team which has learning-based goals may choose to assign some roles to team members who wish to develop skills in the new area. Many teams also find it beneficial to occasionally rotate roles among team members.

2. Use ground rules

In order to be effective, teams need to create a set of clearly defined and agreed to ground rules that reflect how *they* want their team to operate. The emphasis is key: it's the team that needs to decide what is and isn't acceptable. Examples of ground rules include:

- Meetings will start on time
- All viewpoints will be heard
- It's OK for anyone to suggest meeting methods
- If someone can't attend, they need to let the team leader know at least a day in advance
- Cell phones will be turned off
- Prework needs to be sent out at least 2 days in advance
- Any decision related to the direction of this project must be made by consensus

These are just samples; your team needs to decide for itself what practices or behaviors are critical to how you want to work together. How many rules to have is often as much art as it is science. Too few rules and regulations lead to chaos; too many imprisons the team within its own bureaucracy.

Think about ground rules as a way to encourage your team to develop positive habits and/or correct bad habits. That means your rules will evolve over time: The need for a ground rule goes away once the good habits have become ingrained or the bad habits of the team have been eliminated. As your team matures, conduct analyses of why they made mistakes or did not achieve their results; these learnings often become the basis for new ground rules.

For example, a team might have noticed that they often start meetings late because one or more members are not present in the meeting room at the time listed on the agenda. They may decide to set up a ground rule that meetings will start on time whether or not everyone is present, or one that says anyone who shows up late pays a small fine to the team (with all those fines to be used to pay for meeting snacks or a "free lunch" for the team). Another team that thinks discussions seem to ramble and that people make the same basic points repetitively may create a ground rule that it's acceptable for anyone to say "got it" to another team member if and when that person begins to repeat themselves.

Obviously, ground rules such as these should be based on the unanimous agreement of all the team members or they could be viewed as punitive or singling out one individual.

3. Plan

When coming up with this list of team processes, we were tempted to add a noun after the word "Plan," but we couldn't come up with any single term that encompassed all of the kinds of plans that a team needs to do, so we stuck with just the verb.

Top-notch teams plan at so many levels that most of it is second nature. They'll have a master plan for how their project will unfold, documented with a tool like a Gantt chart. When assigning tasks, they'll always talk about the "how" (*Marc, you're going to take charge of collecting data over the next two weeks. How do you think that's going to work and what do you need from the rest of the team?"*). They'll use meeting agendas, which are plans for how their time will be spent. If they need to adjust the agenda, they'll spend a quick 10-seconds on a plan for how to reallocate time (*Ok, even though we're going long, we're going to spend 10 more minutes on this issue then spend 5 minutes summarizing where we are. We'll start the discussion on the next topic, but recognize that we may have to finish it at the next meeting.)*

Why all this planning at so many levels? For a team to be able to improve, it has to know what it *thought* would happen, then compare that initial plan against actual performance to see where they were right and where they could improve. If the anticipated plan and results do not match, the team can then examine why and talk about what they need to do differently next time around.

Resource assessment

In creating their planning documents, effective teams take pains to accurately assess and incorporate all of the resources available to the team into their plans and processes. Key elements assessed are:

Time: How much is available and how much will be required to achieve the goals that have been set. It is particularly important to assess the time commitment of each individual team member. Generally, if someone has less than five hours per week available, it would be wise to replace that team member and make them an advisor or non-core team member. Large discrepancies in time availability versus the amount required should trigger a revision in goals or scope of the project. It is far better to do this at the outset of a project or a meeting than to be forced to undertake adjustments on the fly.

Skills: There are two aspects of a skill inventory: the first is doing a Belbin analysis so you can understand team role strengths, identify surpluses or voids, etc.; the second is surveying the subject matter expertise or functional competencies represented by the core team members. The inventory may show that some skills needed are lacking on the core team, in which case you need to either add someone to the team who has those skills or find someone with the needed skills who you can draw on as needed.

Available data: While the team initially almost never has everything it needs or wants, it is critical to make a formalized survey of what exists prior to commencing the planning process. It is also imperative that the quality of existing data is assessed. Data collection and analysis will be a primary component of any continuous improvement process. The extent of the data gaps will largely determine the duration and complexity of the early data collection phases of the project.

Teams often assess these elements during the project launch (where the focus is on the larger project), but only the best apply the same assessment processes to ongoing team meetings. Making sure team meetings are 100% productive is a key leadership challenge. It is therefore imperative that someone is assigned the responsibility of assessing the data and other requirements that are necessary to have a productive meeting prior to the meeting taking place. If not done, this can lead to great frustration and ultimately derail the larger project. For example, convening a meeting to reach a decision can be folly if the required data is not available, the team lacks a facilitator, or time is not available for substantial debate. Any team-based process, regardless of size or scope, should incorporate an accurate assessment of resources available to the team.

Contingency Planning and Flexibility

Von Moltke, a Prussian army general, once said "no plan of battle ever survives first contact with the enemy." His point was that while it's important to have an initial plan, it is perhaps even more important to be prepared to deviate from it as more information comes to light.

Contingency planning is a critical but often ignored aspect of project planning. Great teams develop multiple courses of action and create fall-back plans. These are invoked as dictated by events and the weaknesses of the initial plan are exposed. Any of the structures discussed above are candidates for coverage by a contingency plan. The most common applications of contingency planning are in time management and which decision-making process to employ.

Great teams establish contingency plans to account for changes in the resources available to them or errors in their initial plans. They decide on alternative courses of action well in advance of entering into their meetings and activities. What happens if they run low on time—will they extend the meeting or adjourn and reconvene later? What happens if they cannot reach a decision using their desired approach—will they insist on discussing until everyone agrees or resort to some tie-breaker or alternative such as majority rule.

The benefits of contingency planning lie both in the predetermined responses and in how it improves the initial plan itself. Often, realizing that the initial design may not work and that a contingency plan is required results in a revision of the main plan which makes the team more effective. Use of contingency plans also combats the need to perfect a plan before taking action. For many teams this type of perfectionism slows them down to such a degree that they become completely ineffective. The contingencies allow them to be comfortable in a "try fast, fail fast, learn fast" mode and ultimately achieve better results.

4. Document and display progress

Documentation serves a variety of purposes. It is a lasting record of not only what decisions the team has made but also the underlying data and rationale behind those decisions. The ultimate goal of documentation lies in the transfer of the team's learning to others in the organization. Within the team, documentation serves primarily to reduce the amount of time spent on rework within a meeting or project: trying to recall who was assigned what tasks, what has been decided, etc. It is also particularly helpful when a team member has missed a meeting and needs to be informed of the proceedings.

There are several basic forms of documentation that good teams employ to be more successful and efficient: agendas, benefits and concerns, parking lots, and action item logs, among others. The key to these items being of use to the team is that they are available in real-time to any of the team members. This implies either a central database for electronic documentation or having the documentation posted during meetings. Many of the most powerful applications of tools or templates in teams derive their power from being publicly visible to all of the team members.

Documentation, when it serves to align team members, is time well spent. Used to excess, it can become merely an administrative burden with few redeeming benefits. The proper amount of documentation can often be tested by measuring whether or not the information being captured and displayed is ever referred back to. If not, good teams will eliminate that portion of their documentation activities.

5. Use feedback

Feedback systems are an essential part of continuous improvement and also of all successful teams. They serve to ensure that mistakes are detected and corrected. Basically, everything a team does is open for feedback, as described by two broad categories:

A) The subject matter of the project
- How good a job did the team do in learning about the process, product, service, problem, etc.?
- Did the team meet its goals?

B) The team processes used to get there
- Meeting effectiveness
- Group interactions
- Data gathering and analysis
- Planning (Did the team follow its plan? What impact did that have, good or bad, on achieving the goals?)

Doing feedback on these issues can occur in three basic styles:

1) **Post-mortem:** As the name implies, this is feedback done after the fact—at the end of the meeting, at the end of the project.

2) **Periodic:** Periodic feedback is conducted at pre-planned intervals. This can be at natural milestones or at some fixed interval (such as every 30 minutes in a meeting, or at the end of each phase in a DMAIC

project). Periodic systems are often integral parts of processes at large companies: personnel performance reviews, quarterly financial reviews, weekly status meetings, inventory audits, etc. Sadly, they are often applied only to the systems of the company, not the interaction within the teams where they could yield perhaps the biggest benefits. For teams, periodic reviews offer a chance to make any midcourse corrections to the team's processes so that they can become more efficient and effective.

3) **Concurrent:** Concurrent feedback is different from periodic only in that it is not pre-scheduled and is generally unstructured. This spontaneous, real-time feedback is rarely seen in newly formed teams. It seems to evolve out of their learning to work better together, perhaps building on what they have learned from their previous mistakes. Concurrent feedback is particularly effective when the team has discussed the main issues it needs to monitor beforehand and permission is granted for team members to note any warning signals they are picking up. Ground rules which become routine often evolve into the focus of concurrent feedback, at which point they may drop off the list of ground rules governing the team.

Time Is of the Essence

The completion of a feedback cycle offers a chance to learn something, so the more frequently this occurs—and the sooner after an error or problem has arisen—faster a team can improve its performance. That's why concurrent or periodic feedback are far more useful than post-mortems.

Creating a feedback plan

As indicated above, feedback can and should happen both spontaneously and as part of a structured, scheduled review. It can take the form of a discussion among the team or written evaluations (followed by discussion). It can be free-form or structured around predefined criteria or focus areas.

For example, one free-form technique is to do a "Benefits and Concerns" (Bs & Cs) check. The team leader simply asks everyone to brainstorm a list of benefits (what went well in the just-concluded session or discussion) and then concerns about how the team performed (areas for potential improvement). This is conducted as a group, with one person scribing the responses on a flipchart as they are spoken.

Table 4.A: Bs & Cs check

Benefits	Concerns
Prework was really helpful	People talked over each other
Started on time	We didn't get to the last agenda item
Susan brought donuts	Ran out of time
Good open debate	We have to transcribe the map on the whiteboard after the meeting
Visual process maps will be great for communication later in project	Need to send agenda out earlier
	Maybe Fred F. should have been here at this meeting

A more structured alternative would be if the team decided that it wanted to do a much better job at, for example, equalizing participation. At the end of the session, team members would be asked to rate every individual's participation, including their own, on a scale of 1 to 5. These subjective rankings could then be the basis for any suggestions for doing better the next time around.

Feedback, like data discovery, is a situation where *none* is the worst possible scenario, *some* is great, and *too much* can leave a team feeling battered and bruised. Don't make it too onerous ("I have a ten-page survey for each of you to fill out") or no one will do it. Many teams find a balance by allotting the last 5 minutes of each meeting to feedback and scheduling longer, more in-depth reviews on team process or project content periodically.

Whatever path you choose, the critical piece is to make sure feedback happens.

Conclusion

The five activities discussed in this chapter—running good meetings, using ground rules, planning, documenting, and using feedback—represent the fundamental building blocks of efficient team operation. Having these processes in place will ensure that your time together will be put to good use, and that you'll get better and better at collaboration as your project proceeds.

CHAPTER 5

Assigning
Responsibilities

For most of us, the following statements and exchanges
sound all too familiar:

Statement: "Did anyone take notes from that discussion?"

Statement: "I can't believe you guys made that decision
without me, when I know more about the current situation than anyone else."

Question: "Do you have that data on the last product
test?"

Answer: "No, I thought you were going to do that. I
just suggested it was something we should do."

Question: "Why is everyone still doing this the old way?"
Answer: "Nobody ever told us to do it differently. I'd
heard a rumor that your team made some changes, but
I never saw any instructions."

These kinds of miscommunications occur all the time in
most teams, but not on high-performing team. This is
another area where a little diligence can have huge payoffs
in team productivity, which is why discussing responsibilities and accountability is second nature on effective teams.

Deciding Who Should Do What

A formal set of structures ensures that everyone on the team understands what needs to be accomplished. The team needs to consider a multitude of factors when deciding who will do what tasks:

- Time available for the tasks
- Personal interest in the task or outcome
- Skills, especially where they are unique
- Balancing workload amongst the team members

As a general rule, teams first assign tasks or roles based on something unique to the individuals on the teams (who is good at something or has experience relevant to the task). Some teams then ask for volunteers to take on the remaining tasks. Most teams seek a balance of overall workload amongst the team members, with any remaining general tasks allocated based on time availability.

As you work through these decisions, keep in mind the insight to be gained from Belbin's work with Team Role Theory. His counsel is to take those individuals with demonstrated aptitude for certain activities, as seen in their top team roles, and line them up with tasks that have those characteristics. One example of this might be the need to have someone on the team perform data analysis. The Monitor Evaluator (ME) role seems to line up well, with an argument to be made that the skills in Completer Finisher (CF) and/or Specialist (SP) would also be somewhat helpful. Choosing someone who had ME as one of their weakest roles would be setting that person up for failure, and by extension setting the team up to fail as well.

Most of the activities that a team will want to assign more permanently to individuals can be quickly assessed as to what Belbin Team Role characteristics would be helpful or harmful to the performance of that activity. We often see a "pick the extremes" approach employed to do this. The critical requirements are determined and the appropriate Belbin roles are given a plus sign; the pitfalls are also identified and given a minus sign. This can be done by looking quickly at the attributes of each of the nine team role descriptions.

For example, an assessment of what it takes to do a great job at conducting customer interviews might lead a team to decide that they ideally want the following profile: +RI, +CF, -SH—a gregarious or extroverted (+RI) and detail oriented (+CF) interviewer who does not try to convince the customer to their own viewpoint (-SH). The team might then decide who on the team best fits this profile and assign them the job, or at least rule out a couple of team members as bad choices for that task.

However, also remember that Belbin's theory allows for an individual to "flex" into a manageable role, as long as that stretch does not have to be maintained continuously for a long period of time. Tasks which are short in duration may not need to be as closely scrutinized for how well they align with the Belbin profile of the individual. Good examples of this are responsibilities that pertain only to a single meeting. Take the meeting role of facilitator; the ideal fit would seem to be someone with strong Coordinator (CO) capabilities, but giving the facilitation role to someone with CO as their number 5 or 6 ranked role may work just fine; the person would probably not be unduly stressed and the team could support and monitor the person making the team role sacrifice. These temporary adjustments are often quite beneficial to the team as it allows the strong CO to drop into other roles during the meeting (providing subject matter expertise or allowing them to more forcefully advocate their own personal views without feeling conflicted by the desire to stay neutral as the facilitator).

Documenting Responsibilities: The RACI Model

The model we recommend for framing and documenting the output of these discussions is called RACI (pronounced "racy"). The letters summarize the four different ways that individuals or groups can be involved in any given activity:

- **Responsible** - people who are expected to actively participate in the activity and contribute to the best of their abilities; they do the work.
- **Accountable** - the person who is ultimately held responsible for the results; they make sure the work gets done by someone.
- **Consulted** - people who either have a particular expertise they can contribute to specific decisions (their advice will be sought) or who must be consulted with for some other reason *before* a final decision is made (for example, someone in finance often consults on internal projects to help quantify costs or gains).

- **Informed** - people who are affected by the activity/decision and therefore need to be kept informed, but do not participate in the effort (they are usually notified of the outcome after the final decisions are made).

Figure 5.1: Sample RACI Chart

	Senior Execs	Project Sponsor	Green Belt	Team members	Finance Rep	Master BB
Draft a Project Charter	A	R				
Evaluate the Charter	A	C			C	R
Revise the Charter	A	R			C	
Authorize Launch of the Project	A,R	C	I			I
Choose Team Members		A,R	R	C		
Notify Team Members		A,R	I	I		
Send out Team Launch prework		A	R	I		
Conduct a Team Launch event		C	A,R	C		
Collect Data			A	R		
Analyze Data		I	A,R	C		C
Develop Solutions	I	C	A,R	R		

One application of this type of thinking is to complete a RACI chart (an example is given in a few pages) at the beginning of the project (or at any significant milestone) to:

- Document responsibilities within the team
- Make sure that there is an accountability for every key action
- Resolve any overlaps or gaps in responsibilities

This upfront RACI work should be part of every team's planning stage.

Equally important, however, is that a team should use RACI on-the-fly, discussing responsibilities whenever new actions get assigned. It's not necessary to update the RACI chart every time, but your team documentation should reflect any RACI decisions or revisions the team makes.

Initial Assignment of Responsibilities

1. **Identify activities or tasks, and write them down the side of a matrix (as the row headings).**

   - EX: evaluate, schedule, write, record, determine, operate, monitor, prepare, update, collect, approve, conduct, develop, inspect, train, publish, report, and review

   - Avoid obvious or generic activities (EX: "attend meetings")

   - When the action verb implies a judgment or decision (e.g., evaluate, monitor, inspect, review), add a phrase to indicate the primary outcome. EX: "Evaluate test film to identify defects"

2. **List team members across the top of the matrix (as the column headings).**

3. **Fill in the RACI chart**

   For each activity, determine who must be involved. Enter an R, A, C, I, or leave it blank as appropriate. The goal is not to completely fill in all the squares in the matrix. Rather it is to keep the filled-in squares to a minimum while ensuring that the tasks will be completed and that those who need to be involved in decisions will be.

Apply your Belbin insights

Remember, when determining which team member should be responsible or accountable for a certain activity, be sure to apply the lessons learned from your Belbin team roles analysis. Have someone with Plant or Resource Investigator strengths take the lead in developing creative ideas. Put a Completer Finisher in charge of details. Hopefully, your team leader will have strong Coordinator tendencies—if not, he or she will need a lot of help from some who does.

4. Review the task assignments (looking across rows); adjust as needed.

> **There is at least one R.** If there are no Rs, the job *may not* get done because no one feels responsible. team members may be waiting to approve, be consulted, or informed; no one sees their role as being the one to take the initiative.

> **There should be one and only one A.** There must be one and only one A per task. Accountability should be pushed down to the most suitable level. Having more than one A will lead to confusion about who is running the show; it can lead to finger pointing and missed task completion.

> **Keep Cs to a minimum.** Every C will require consultation before a decision gets made. If there are lots of Cs, it may be time-consuming and cumbersome to make decisions. Do all these people need to be consulted? Are there justifiable benefits in consulting all of them?

> **Minimize the number of I's.** Do all the Is need to be routinely informed or only in exceptional cir-

cumstances? If the person with an I in the RACI chart is not going to change anything they do after being informed, remove the I from their square.

5. **Review workload for each person (looking down the columns); adjust as needed. You want to make sure that for each column (person) the task load is reasonable.** Overloading a person or group with work will lead to failure. It may be necessary to spread some of the Rs around a bit more widely.

6. **Get feedback and buy-in**
   - Review the initial draft of the RACI chart with the team and other groups or people represented on the chart
   - Negotiate agreement on and commitment to roles and responsibilities as laid out in the chart

7. **Periodically review and revise the chart**
   - As the project progresses, review the chart and update it as needed

Using RACI On-the-Fly

The RACI terminology can also be used in an informal way without resorting to the creation of an explicit chart. Some teams will simply make sure that action items or activities are always handed out with at least the R and the A specified. One example of this use of RACI might be the end of a meeting:

"So we definitely need to go get some data from the purchasing department. Who's going to do that? OK, it looks like Todd has the R, and I will take the A. Todd, can you call me on Thursday with an update on the status of the data collection after you have met with those guys?"

Conclusion

Being absolutely clear about who is going to do what by when is simply a given on high-performance teams. The RACI format helps teams work through those issues upfront as part of its planning work. And, equally important, it provides the basis for review and improvement. A complete RACI chart is the expression of what a team *wants* to have happen; it is a hypothesis, a speculative design of how the team will work together. Should the team struggle or fail, then the team can reassess its RACI chart to see if there is a better alternative for the way the team is organized.

By using the RACI chart to perform a post-mortem analysis of team performance, a variety of issues may be surfaced.

Individuals who were assigned an R for an activity that did not get completed can be made aware of the underperformance. In the same way, the person who had the A for that same task should share culpability for the task not getting completed. What is absolutely critical in this type of analysis (or any form of feedback) is that the root cause of the failure be determined and corrected. Attributing blame is largely counterproductive.

Appendix

Interpreting a Belbin Report

ASSESSMENT RESULTS IN RANK ORDER

Name Kevin Carson
Organisation 3Circle Partners
Department

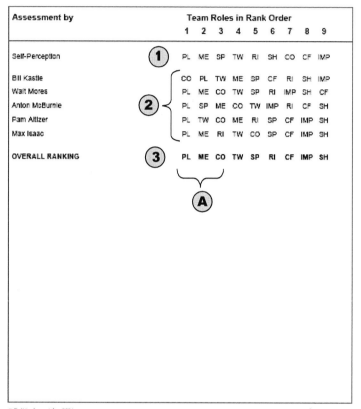

Assessment by	Team Roles in Rank Order								
	1	2	3	4	5	6	7	8	9
Self-Perception (1)	PL	ME	SP	TW	RI	SH	CO	CF	IMP
Bill Kastle	CO	PL	TW	ME	SP	CF	RI	SH	IMP
Walt Mores	PL	ME	CO	TW	SP	RI	IMP	SH	CF
Anton McBurnie (2)	PL	SP	ME	CO	TW	IMP	RI	CF	SH
Pam Altizer	PL	TW	CO	ME	RI	SP	CF	IMP	SH
Max Isaac	PL	ME	RI	TW	CO	SP	CF	IMP	SH
OVERALL RANKING (3)	PL	ME	CO	TW	SP	RI	CF	IMP	SH

(A)

Page 1: Overall Summary

How to Read This Page

Lists the nine roles in rank order from 1 = strongest to 9 = weakest in three groupings:

SELF (Area 1) - The top line is based only on your own responses to the self-assessment form.

OBSERVERS (Area 2) - The following lines translate each observer's responses into the roles they see you playing. Observer names have been included to provide context for the results, but the raw data of their responses is hidden from you. (You cannot tell if they said you were "professional," "aggressive," fussy," etc.)

OVERALL (Area 3) - The overall ranking is basically a weighted average of all the lines above as calculated by very complex formulas within the Belbin software system. It is over-weighted towards the observers on the premise that they are more accurate than you may be yourself.

Areas to Investigate

Concentrate on the top two or three roles from the overall ranking (last line, Area A). Look at where these roles fall for each observer. Generally, it is preferable for the top roles to always fall in the top half for all the observers, as this indicates consistency in behavior. The greater the agreement across and among the observers, the more consistently your behavior is being perceived.

Pie Chart of SPI versus Observer Data

Name Kevin Carson
Organisation 3Circle Partners
Department

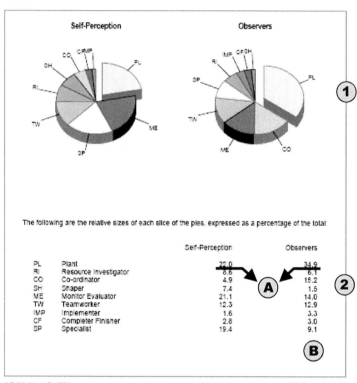

Self-Perception   Observers

The following are the relative sizes of each slice of the pies, expressed as a percentage of the total:

		Self-Perception	Observers
PL	Plant	22.0	34.9
RI	Resource Investigator	8.6	6.1
CO	Co-ordinator	4.9	15.2
SH	Shaper	7.4	1.5
ME	Monitor Evaluator	21.1	14.0
TW	Teamworker	12.3	12.9
IMP	Implementer	1.6	3.3
CF	Completer Finisher	2.8	3.0
SP	Specialist	19.4	9.1

Printed on 28-Jan-03

Page 2: Pie Charts

How to Read This Page

This page compares the SELF and OBSERVER perceptions of what roles the report subject is playing.

The top section (Area 1) displays the scores for the nine roles in a pie chart format, self-perception on the left and a composite of observers' reactions on the right.

The bottom section (Area 2) expresses the results numerically, with the totals of each column equaling 100. These numbers correspond to the sizes of the pie slices above.

Areas to Investigate

Test for coherence by comparing the two columns of figures at the bottom of the page. If you notice any differences of 10.0 or more (in either direction), these are "disconnects" and indicate a potential lack of coherence (meaning you see yourself differently from how others see you). *In the example at left, the roles PL (see comparison "A"), CO and SP have difference of 10 or more points.*

Test for how distinct your role-playing is by examining the Observer data at the bottom of the page (labeled "B"). Clear strengths and weaknesses will show up as a mix of some higher numbers (16.0 or higher) and some lower scores (less than 5.0). If all the scores are relatively equal to each other, this may indicate that the observers are not getting a clear picture of what your preferred roles are.

SELF-PERCEPTION TEAM ROLE PROFILE

Name Kevin Carson
Organisation 3Circle Partners
Department

BELBIN		Least Preferred Roles			Manageable Roles				Preferred Roles					Roles and Descriptions	Team-Role Contribution	Allowable Weaknesses
		0	10	20	30	40	50	60	70	80	90	100			
PL												X	Plant	Creative, imaginative, unorthodox. Solves difficult problems.	Ignores incidentals. Too pre-occupied with own thoughts to communicate effectively.
RI						X							Resource Investigator	Extrovert, enthusiastic, communicative. Explores opportunities. Develops contacts.	Over-optimistic. Can lose interest once initial enthusiasm has passed.
CO				X									Co-ordinator	Mature, confident. Clarifies goals. Brings other people together to promote team discussions.	Can be seen as manipulative. Offloads personal work.
SH					X								Shaper	Challenging, dynamic, thrives on pressure. Has the drive and courage to overcome obstacles.	Prone to provocation. Liable to offend others.
ME											X		Monitor Evaluator	Serious-minded, strategic and discerning. Sees all options. Judges accurately.	Can lack drive and ability to inspire others.
TW							X						Teamworker	Co-operative, mild, perceptive and diplomatic. Listens, builds, averts friction.	Indecisive in crunch situations.
IMP			X										Implementer	Disciplined, reliable, conservative in habits. A capacity for taking practical steps and actions.	Somewhat inflexible. Slow to respond to new possibilities.
CF			X										Completer Finisher	Painstaking, conscientious, anxious. Searches out errors and omissions. Delivers on time.	Inclined to worry unduly. Reluctant to let others into their job.
SP										X			Specialist	Single-minded, self-starting, dedicated. Provides knowledge and skills in rare supply.	Contributes on only a limited front. Dwells on specialised personal interests.

Points dropped: 3 out of 70

Page 3: Your Relative Self-Perception Scores

How to Read This Page

This page is based *only* on the SELF assessment responses; no observer data has been used. It converts your responses into a score for each role on a scale from 0 to 100.

The scale is based on how your responses compare to those of everyone else in the Belbin software database. A score of 100 would indicate that you gave yourself more points for that role than anyone else in the database, a score of 0 would indicate that no one else was lower than you.

The page is divided somewhat arbitrarily into three sections which correspond to preferred, manageable, and least preferred roles. It is generally preferable to have a few roles in each of the three sections. Profiles which have all nine roles clustered right down the middle may indicate that you have an indistinct view of your strengths and weaknesses from a Belbin Team Role standpoint.

Note: The role descriptions on the right-hand side of this page are a handy reference for remembering what each role means.

BAR GRAPH OF OBSERVER WORDS

Name Kevin Carson
Organisation 3Circle Partners
Department

BELBIN		Team-Role Contribution	Roles and Descriptions	Allowable Weaknesses
PL	Plant	Creative, imagination, unorthodox. Solves difficult problems.	Ignores incidentals. Too pre-occupied with own thoughts to communicate effectively.
RI	Resource Investigator	Extrovert, enthusiastic, communicative. Explores opportunities. Develops contacts.	Over-optimistic. Can lose interest once initial enthusiasm has passed.
CO	Co-ordinator	Mature, confident. Clarifies goals. Brings other people together to promote team discussions.	Can be seen as manipulative. Offloads personal work.
SH	Shaper	Challenging, dynamic, thrives on pressure. Has the drive and courage to overcome obstacles.	Prone to provocation. Liable to offend others.
ME	Monitor Evaluator	Serious minded, strategic and discerning. Sees all options. Judges accurately.	Can lack drive and ability to inspire others.
TW	Teamworker	Co-operative, mild, perceptive and diplomatic. Listens, builds, averts friction.	Indecisive in crunch situations.
IMP	Implementer	Disciplined, reliable, conservative in habits. A capacity for taking practical steps and actions.	Somewhat inflexible. Slow to respond to new possibilities.
CF	Completer Finisher	Painstaking, conscientious, anxious. Searches out errors and omissions. Delivers on time.	Inclined to worry unduly. Reluctant to let others into own job.
SP	Specialist	Single-minded, self-starting, dedicated. Provides knowledge and skills in rare supply.	Contributes on only a limited front. Dwells on specialised personal interests.

Page 4: Positive vs. Negative Weighting

How to Read This Page

This page is based *only* on the OBSERVER responses. The report totals up all of the observer responses which correspond to the various roles and displays the results as a series of bar graphs.

Each bar is composed of a positive and a negative component. If you look at the page horizontally, positive attributesare shown to the right of the line indicated by the line labeled "1," negatives to the left of it.

The overall length of any given bar (both the positive and negative components) represents the extent to which you are seen to play that role. It shows *how much* the role is seen to be played. The ratio of positive to negative components within any given bar represents how adept you are at playing that role. It shows *how well* the role is being played.

Areas to Investigate

Test for disallowable weaknesses by examining the ratio of positive to negative in each bar (area 1). If the ratio is less than 5:1, it is an indication that the role is not being well-received by the observers. The simplest strategy to correct this is to reduce the extent to which the role is played (do it less), which usually restores the ratio to an acceptable level. *In this sample report, there are no disallowable weaknesses.*

Note: You should not try to correct or eliminate the negative portions of the bars *unless* they are disallowable. Tolerate them because they are linked to the strengths you see.

COUNSELLING REPORT

Name Kevin Carson
Organisation 3Circle Partners
Department

Please note that this report is based on the complete profile.

Your profile shows that you are a strong thinking type. One of your assets is your ability to weigh up the options and choose the best course of action. With your independent outlook you are also well placed to come up with new and original ideas. This means that you are most likely to make your mark in an area where the problems are complex and difficult. The ideal situation could be a planning, design or trouble-shooting function. When you work with busy executives, however, there is some risk that you will be seen as standing for all thought and no action. Do not be tempted into a general debate that can lead to "paralysis by analysis." Avoid working with too many thinking type colleagues. Choose practical subordinates who work on issues that may be important but which you are likely to find tedious.

Unless you are able to function as an independent person, the relationship with your boss will be an all important issue. It is likely that you will work best for someone who excels at interpersonal communications and who appreciates advice. Where others are concerned try to exercise your influence on a one-to-one basis and on the broader front let others do any missionary work on your behalf.

Your operating style is closest to that of strategic leadership, which is usually available only at senior positions. However, before such an opportunity could present itself, you are likely to need credibility at the operational level. That might pose problems in your case. Possibly, you would be well advised to make a team-role sacrifice by dealing as effectively as you can with issues that don't excite you. That may be the necessary prelude to reaching the position to which in the long run you are best suited. The good news is that the longer you survive, the more likely you are to become a valued contribution and to gain the greatest sense of personal fulfilment.

Your own perception of your top team role is supported by the views of others.

On a final note, you need to take account of the role for which you are least suited. You do not appear to have the characteristics of the hard-driving executive who obtains results by power and pressure. If you can work in harmony with someone who has these complementary qualities, your own performance is likely to improve.

Page 5: Counseling Report

How to Read This Page

This page is based on the complete profile. The statements it contains have been compiled based on interviews with numerous people who have Belbin profiles similar to yours. As a result, you will likely find many items of interest to you about where you can be most successful or where you should exercise caution.

The descriptions contained in this narrative are based on the overall rankings from the bottom of the first page. Specifically, it is based on the top two roles and the very last role (thus roles number 1, 2, and 9 on the last line of page 1).

Note: The descriptions on this page are directionally correct, not "gospel." The accuracy of this page typically improves once a consistent and coherent profile emerges.

MOST HIGHLY RATED OBSERVER RESPONSES

BELBIN

Name	Kevin Carson
Organisation	3Circle Partners
Department	

This list shows words from Observers Assessments and their scores in descending order of popularity.

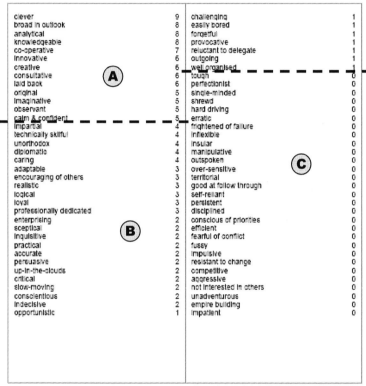

clever	9	challenging	1
broad in outlook	8	easily bored	1
analytical	8	forgetful	1
knowledgeable	8	provocative	1
co-operative	7	reluctant to delegate	1
innovative	6	outgoing	1
creative	6	well organised	1
consultative	6	tough	0
laid back	6	perfectionist	0
original	5	single-minded	0
imaginative	5	shrewd	0
observant	5	hard driving	0
calm & confident	5	erratic	0
impartial	4	frightened of failure	0
technically skilful	4	inflexible	0
unorthodox	4	insular	0
diplomatic	4	manipulative	0
caring	4	outspoken	0
adaptable	3	over-sensitive	0
encouraging of others	3	territorial	0
realistic	3	good at follow through	0
logical	3	self-reliant	0
loyal	3	persistent	0
professionally dedicated	3	disciplined	0
enterprising	2	conscious of priorities	0
sceptical	2	efficient	0
inquisitive	2	fearful of conflict	0
practical	2	fussy	0
accurate	2	impulsive	0
persuasive	2	resistant to change	0
up-in-the-clouds	2	competitive	0
critical	2	aggressive	0
slow-moving	2	not interested in others	0
conscientious	2	unadventurous	0
indecisive	2	empire building	0
opportunistic	1	impatient	0

Page 6: Observer Responses

How to Read This Page

This page lists the actual words checked off by the observers on their assessment forms. All of the individual observers' responses have been added together to create this summary. This page represents the detail behind the bar charts represented on page 4 of the report.

Each observer was given instructions to check any phrases which are representative of you, and to "double check" a few phrases which are very, very much typical of what they see you doing. Thus, the maximum score for any phrase on this sheet is twice the number of observers. *Since this person had 5 observers, the maximum score would be 10.*

Areas to Investigate

Break the report into three sections. Section A represents the "unanimous" attributes. The cutoff score for this section will be equal to the number of observers you had (anything above 5 in this example).

Section B consists of scores from 1 to the cutoff above. This represents attributes occasionally seen.

Section C is comprised of attributes never seen; they have scores of 0.